Knitting
Ephemera
⋙→

Knitting Ephemera

A Compendium
of ARTICLES,
Useful and Otherwise,
for the Edification and
AMUSEMENT *of the*
Handknitter

Carol J. Sulcoski

sixth&springbooks
NEW YORK

sixth&springbooks 161 Avenue of the Americas New York, NY 10013

Library of Congress Cataloging-in-Publication Data
Sulcoski, Carol, 1965- author, editor.
 Knitting ephemera : a compendium of articles,
useful and otherwise, for the edification and
amusement of the handknitter / by Carol J. Sulcoski.
-- First Edition.
     pages cm
ISBN 978-1-936096-98-5 (hardback)
1. Knitting--Miscellanea. I. Title.
 TT820.S933 2016
 746.43'2--dc23

PRINTED IN CHINA

Publishing Director
Joan Krellenstein

Managing Editor
Laura Cooke

Creative Director
Diane Lamphron

Editorial Assistant
Jacob Siefert

....

*Vice President /
Editorial Director*
Trisha Malcolm

Publisher
Caroline Kilmer

Production Manager
David Joinnides

President
Art Joinnides

Chairman
Jay Stein

For knitters
everywhere, in
appreciation
of all you have
brought to my life.

THE PATRON SAINT OF **KNITTING**

THE CATHOLIC ENCYCLOPEDIA DEFINES A PATRON SAINT AS "one who has been assigned by a venerable tradition, or chosen by election, as a special intercessor with God and the proper advocate of a particular locality." Patron saints have been designated for everything from medical conditions and natural disasters to professions, activities, and social causes. There is a patron saint for shepherds (St. Bernadette of Lourdes); needleworkers (St. Clare, an Italian saint renowned for her skills at embroidery); and wool workers and combers (St. Blaise, who got the honor because he was tortured with steel combs, which resemble carding combs—ouch!). So who is the patron saint for knitters?

ALAS, NO SAINT HAS OFFICIALLY BEEN DESIGNATED PATRON SAINT OF KNITTING, although there are a few strong contenders. St. Fiacre is commonly mentioned as a potential candidate for the patron saint of knitters. ST. FIACRE was a monk who lived in the seventh century; some sources say he was born in Ireland, others that he was from Scotland. Either way, he traveled to what is now France to do missionary work. There is no obvious connection between the stories of his life and knitting; indeed, many sources suggest he bore an antipathy toward women, barring them from his monastery. (And it is this aversion to women that some believe caused him to be named patron saint of venereal disease sufferers!). Some sources claim that in the Middle Ages, a Paris guild of knitters or tailors designated St. Fiacre as their patron saint; hence his association with the craft.

ST. SEBASTIAN, who was martyred in the third century, is sometimes mentioned as the patron saint of knitters. St. Sebastian was sentenced to be shot to death by archers, but the arrows miraculously did not kill him; he survived, only to be beaten to death later by his oppressors. St. Sebastian's gory connection with knitting is based on the arrows that are symbolic of his martyrdom, the shape of which resemble knitting needles.

ST. DYMPHNA is also sometimes mentioned as a suitable candidate for the patron saint of knitters. Legend says that when Dymphna's mother—a devout Christian—died, her pagan father sought to marry a woman who resembled his deceased wife. When he could not find such a woman, he began to look lasciviously at his own daughter. Dymphna would have none of it, so her father beheaded her. (Not many happy endings in the legends of the saints, unfortunately.) St. Dymphna is well known as the patron saint of those with mental and nervous disorders, but certainly that has no connection to her designation as the possible patron saint of knitters!

ST. JOHN VIANNEY is one of the few saints with a tangible connection to knitting, or at least wool: as a child, he tended his father's sheep on the family farm. ST. LUCY is sometimes mentioned as another potential patron saint for knitters, but perhaps this is because she is patron saint of those with eye troubles, a potential hazard for those who knit too much. ✳

The world record for
largest knitting needles used for knitting
is held by Jeanette Huisinga of the United States. Huisinga knit a gauge swatch (measuring 10 stitches by 10 rows) using 13-foot-long, 3¼-inch-wide needles.

• • • • • • •

The world's ## largest crochet hook measured 6 feet, 1½ inches long, with a diameter of 3 inches. Both record-setting implements were made by Jim Bolin and measured in May 2013 at Monroe Elementary School in Casey, Illinois.

The knitters of Orenburg in Russia
have long been renowned for their beautiful gossamer shawls. Orenburg lace expert Galina Khmeleva tells of a Russian legend in which a Cossack woman knitted a lace shawl and presented it to Catherine the Great. Catherine was so impressed with the exquisite lacework that she paid the knitter a large enough sum to allow the knitter to live the rest of her life in comfort. But the empress wanted to be the only woman in the world to wear such a shawl, so she then had the woman blinded, reasoning that she could then no longer knit shawls. Fortunately for the world, the knitter had a daughter who was also able to knit, and so the tradition of Orenburg shawl knitting survives today.

❖ ❖ ❖ ❖ ❖

Oomingmak means **"the bearded one"** in the Eskimo language—and refers to the Alaskan musk ox, a shaggy animal that survived the Ice Age. The musk ox is neither an ox, strictly speaking, nor musky, but more closely related to sheep and goats. The musk ox was indigenous to Alaska but became extinct there in the mid-19th century. In the 1930s, musk oxen from Greenland were reintroduced to Alaska for domestication, but the project was abandoned, and the remaining oxen ran wild on Nunivak Island. Then, in the 1950s, an anthropologist named John J. Teal began exploring the possibility that qiviut, the downy undercoat of the musk ox, might be used for its fiber. Over the course of many years, he developed a successful breeding program using calves from Nunivak Island in order to harvest their qiviut.

Today, fiberistas know qiviut as a true luxury fiber—rare, expensive, warm, and incredibly soft. Qiviut (pronounced "ki-vee-oot") is extremely fine and on par with superfine fibers such as cashmere and vicuña. It is technically a hair rather than a wool, and it will not shrink. While qiviut has good tensile strength, it is not as durable as many other fibers, and for that reason it is often blended with other, stronger fibers to resist wear. Unlike sheep, musk oxen are not shorn—their qiviut is either plucked or combed from their undercoats, or gathered from objects that the oxen brush against during their molts.

Qiviut does not have a lot of oil in the fiber, unlike wool, but it is extremely warm. Due to its scarcity, yarns and finished items made with qiviut are sold at quite a premium; handknit qiviut scarves can sell for several hundred dollars each, and a single skein of yarn made of 100 percent qiviut fiber can cost between $50 and $90 or more depending on the yarn's quality, thickness, and yardage. ✳

■ ■ ■ HOW DID **WEBS**, A MASSACHUSETTS-BASED YARN COMPANY WITH A MAJOR INTERNET PRESENCE, get lucky enough to scoop up the domain name yarn.com? Art Elkins, who founded WEBS along with his wife, Barbara, was a business professor who joined the WEBS workforce after he retired. "Art read that this thing called the Internet was coming," his daughter-in-law Kathy Elkins recalls, "and the article advised business owners to reserve a URL for their business. I don't even know how he did it. There was no Internet so it wasn't like he could just go online and sign up!" Elkins initially tried to reserve the URL webs.com, but it was already taken. So he opted for yarn.com instead. The rest is history.

What type of garment has most frequently made
the cover of *Vogue Knitting*?
THE PULLOVER SWEATER.
The color most often used for the cover garment?
Believe it or not, WHITE.

Was there a **REAL MARY MAXIM?**

Sort of. In 1952, in a small town in Canada, a couple named Willard
and Olive McPhedrain started a business making and selling spinning
wheels along with a woolen mill manufacturing blankets and work
socks. The mill was so successful that the McPhedrains started a
mail-order company. The business continued to grow, and Willard
McPhedrain sought to create a more personal connection by giving the
company a woman's name. He picked "Mary Maxim," a name inspired
by an employee named Mary Maximchuck. The business continued to
grow, and soon the McPhedrains added an American headquarters. The
company's classic sweaters, with front zips and nature-inspired motifs,
gained a following of their own, being worn over the years by celebrities
like Bob Hope and, more recently, indie rock group Barenaked Ladies.

≫→ THE WORLD'S FIRST REAL SYNTHETIC FIBER WAS
NYLON, first produced in 1939 by the DuPont Company. Dr. Wallace
Carothers and his colleagues at DuPont were experimenting with
polymers (certain chemical structures) and discovered a very strong
polymer that could be shaped into a fiber. After much trial and error,
Carothers chose a polyamide structure that was sturdy enough for
commercial development. DuPont selected its target market—women's
hosiery—and secretly sent a sample batch of nylon to a commercial
knitting mill. (It's said that concern for secrecy was so high that the
chemist who delivered that sample batch slept with the nylon clutched
in his hand on the train!) By 1940, stockings made of nylon were
introduced to the market, and women lined up to buy them. Within
two years, DuPont's nylon had cornered nearly a third of the market
for women's hosiery. The usefulness of nylon to the war effort—it was
used for items like parachutes, tents, and netting—meant that DuPont
had to divert its entire nylon production to the military for a few years.
When nylon stockings became available again after the war, there was
a frenzy as people tried to get their hands (and legs) on the limited
number of pairs available.

Before there were cowls and wristers, there were...

Antimacassars
Small cloths placed over the backs of chairs or sofas to shield them from hair oil

Matinee Coats
Either women's lingerie jackets or baby coats to be worn outside

Semmits
Scottish undershirts

Fascinators
Originally fine, lacy head coverings that hung down on both sides, often adorned with feathers

Polkas
Women's tight-fitting knitted jackets

Berthes
Deep collars tucked in the front of a low-necked dress

Cephalines
Knitted caps

Balaclavas
Knitted helmets that covered the entire head—including ears, hair, and neck—with openings for eyes and nose

Paletots
Short, loose coats that buttoned in front

Muffetees
Small fingerless wristers

SHEEP-Y FACTOIDS

• Sheep have good memories. Some scientists estimate they can remember people or events for up to two years.

• President Woodrow Wilson kept a flock of sheep at the White House after the United States entered World War I, allowing them to graze on the lawn as a symbol of support for the country's war efforts. The sheep's wool was sold to raise money for the war, and their grazing saved money on groundskeeping costs.

• A single sheep can produce up to 30 pounds of wool per year, depending on its breed and other factors, but the average sheep in America produces only 7.3 pounds of wool annually.

• The Navajo name for sheep is *dibé*, which means "that by which we live."

• There are an estimated 1,000+ breeds of sheep in the world, with about 50 of those found in the United States.

The most *expensive knitting yarn* is probably vicuña, a member of the camelid family (which makes it a cousin to the alpaca and llama). Vicuñas are wild animals and live in the highest regions of the Andes Mountains. They produce very fine fiber—about 12 microns. (To give you a basis for comparison, cashmere averages around 16 microns and merino averages 18–24 microns.) Unfortunately, the vicuña produces very small amounts of this fiber and can be shorn only once every three years. At the time this book went to press, 100 percent vicuña yarn was selling for $299.95 per 1-ounce ball. (That's about 217 yards of laceweight yarn.) Runner-up in the budget-buster contest: qiviut, a fiber from the Arctic musk ox, which at the time of this writing sold at just under $96 per 1-ounce/217-yard ball.

Baseball's got the World Series, tennis has Wimbledon, but where does an ace sheep shearer go to test his mettle?
WHY, THE GOLDEN SHEARS COMPETITION, OF COURSE.

In 1958, a group of sheep-shearing enthusiasts from the Wairarapa district of New Zealand set up a competition and invited shearers from all over New Zealand to compete. The competition was such a success that the organizers decided to make it an annual event. They selected the title "Golden Shears," and from 1960 onward the competition has been held to honor excellence in the art of shearing and woolhandling. The United Kingdom and Australia began sponsoring their own Golden Shears competitions, and in 1980 the Golden Shears World Council was established. Today, 13 member countries belong to the World Council, which sponsors a world championship described as "the Olympics of sheep-shearing." The 2015 Golden Shears World Sheep Shearing and Woolhandling Championships were held March 5–7 in Masterton, New Zealand. The winner of the 2015 Golden Shears Open was a Scottish shearer named Gavin Mutch.

In 1850, menswear company D.H. Brooks & Co. changed its name to Brooks Brothers and adopted its famous Golden Fleece logo featuring a sheep suspended by a ribbon. The image had been used in Britain to signify woolen wares during a time when a large portion of the population was illiterate. The Brooks brothers wanted their logo to hark back to the long sartorial history of Europe.

PROVERBIAL WISDOM

● ● ●

A leap year is never a good sheep year.
– ENGLISH PROVERB

Go to the law for a sheep and lose your cow.
– GERMAN PROVERB

Without the shepherd, sheep are not a flock.
– RUSSIAN PROVERB

The quarrel of the sheep doesn't concern the goats.
– AFRICAN PROVERB

An army of sheep led by a lion would defeat an
army of lions led by a sheep.
– ARAB PROVERB

Better to give the wool away than the sheep.
– ITALIAN PROVERB

Eagles fly alone, but sheep flock together.
– POLISH PROVERB

Every family has its black sheep.
– AMERICAN PROVERB

It's a poor sheep that cannot carry its own wool.
– GERMAN PROVERB

● ● ●

⟫⟫→ YOU MIGHT THINK THAT LIGHT-UP KNITTING NEEDLES ARE A RECENT INVENTION. YOU'D BE WRONG. As early as 1918, a Philadelphia woman named Henrietta Kelsey submitted a patent application for knitting needles with luminous points. Kelsey's application described her method as "applying a luminous material, either internally or externally at the region of the point of the needle, with provision for protecting the same against wear occasioned by extensive usage." She suggested that the needle be shaped like a tube, with the luminous material applied inside throughout.

Kelsey's patent application coincided with the knitting frenzy that accompanied World War I. Interestingly, the idea of illuminated needles surfaced again during World War II when a 1944 patent application for a battery-operated illuminated needle stated, "[D]ue to present war conditions, it may be desirable for a knitter to continue knitting during black-outs, real or practice, and to be able to see the work without the use of any light discernible more than a few feet away."

Times have changed, and recent patent applications seeking to further develop light-up knitting needles have cited more personal considerations. A 2006 application for internally illuminated needles states, "Knitting and crocheting are old tasks that have largely been

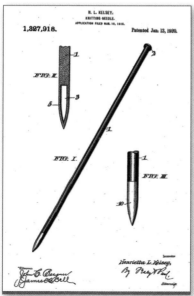

taken over by mechanized production. However, many individuals take care and pride in personally knitting and crocheting pieces by hand. These practices, although centuries old, have consistently been accompanied by the same complaint, a lack of good working light." Those seeking to add a bit of science-fiction pizzazz to their knitting can even find instructions for creating "light saber knitting needles" on various DIY websites. ✴

On February 1, 2015, the

five-millionth

person registered for the online
knitting and crochet site
Ravelry.com.

As of February 2014, Ravelry's
message boards (called forums)
contained over 100 million
individual posts, made up of five
billion words. Designers have
published more than

223,350 patterns

for download via Ravelry.

COMBINING
DIFFERENT COLORED
YARNS IS A TRICKY JOB,
particularly when you're
working with one or more
handpainted yarns. Get a rough
sense of whether your two
color choices work together
by wrapping them around a
large knitting needle or ruler,
alternating colors every
few wraps. You'll be able to
envision how the yarns look next
to each other before casting on or
quickly compare different color
combinations before selecting
one to swatch.

HOW TO TELL THE DIFFERENCE BETWEEN AN ALPACA AND A LLAMA

• An alpaca has shorter, spear-shaped ears, while a llama has longer, banana-shaped ears.

• Alpacas are smaller (approximately 100–175 pounds when full grown), while llamas are often twice the size of a typical alpaca (approximately 200–400 pounds).

• An alpaca has softer, finer hair, since it was bred for centuries to produce luxury fiber; a llama has coarser guard hair befitting its role as pack animal.

We call it crochet, *perhaps derived from the French words* croc *or* croche, *meaning "little hook."* The craft is known as *haken* in the Netherlands, *virkning* in Sweden, *tejer* in Spain, *hekle* in Norway, *hækling* in Denmark, *häkeln* in Germany, *há kování* in the Czech Republic, *uncinetto* in Italy, *virkkaus* in Finland, *gantsilyo* in the Philippines, *szydełkowa* in Poland, and *tambort* in Latvia.

In her book Folk Shawls, *knitwear designer CHERYL OBERLE tells of a piece of Irish folklore that claims if a master knitter puts knitting needles in a baby's hands, the baby will become a good knitter.*

EACH YEAR, FASHIONISTAS—AND YARN COMPANIES—
EAGERLY AWAIT THE RELEASE OF THE PANTONE COLOR
OF THE YEAR. But long before Pantone, there was Margaret Hayden
Rorke, considered by many to be the first professional color forecaster
in America. Rorke, a former actress and suffragette, was named head
of the Textile Color Card Association in 1919. The TCCA (now
known as The Color Assocation of the United States) is a trade group
seeking to provide uniform color forecasting and standardized colors
for the textile industry. Rorke led the TCCA for more than 40 years,
frequently traveling to Paris to take in runway shows and recognizing
the importance of color-coordinating various pieces of a woman's
wardrobe—dress, hat, shoes, gloves—throughout different segments
of the ready-to-wear industry. (Television fans may be familiar with
Rorke's actor son, who most famously played Dr. Bellows on the
sitcom *I Dream of Jeannie*.)

According to Regina Blaszczyk, author of *The Color Revolution*,
even before Rorke's push for standardized colors, French textile mills
had created the first color cards. Based in part on the foldout cards
created by German dyehouses to display their ranges of colors, the
French color cards were released twice yearly and often contained
loops of dyed thread arranged in complementary color combinations.
American retailers and textile companies imported the color cards and
used them to guide their choices for each season's offerings. ✳

➤ A British nobleman named FitzRoy Somerset served in the British
military for many years. Somerset first made a name for himself
fighting in the Napoleonic Wars and taking part in many key battles,
including the Battle of Waterloo, where injuries required the amputation
of his right arm. When the Crimean War broke out in 1853, Somerset
was named commander of the British troops—even though he'd never
led troops in the field and was 65 years old. The results were disastrous,
and Somerset died in 1855 after the British suffered terrible losses in
the Siege of Sevastopol. Somerset's contribution to the knitting world,
according to the Oxford English dictionary, was a new style of
jacket with a diagonal seam running from underarm to collar, a style
that Somerset was known to wear due to the loss of his arm.
We know it as the "raglan" sleeve, as FitzRoy Somerset's title was
LORD OF RAGLAN.

KNITTING MEETS
MURDER

A SELECTION OF MYSTERY NOVELS IN
WHICH KNITTING PLAYS A ROLE

THE MISS MARPLE SERIES BY AGATHA CHRISTIE:
Amateur detective Miss Marple is always knitting, but her knitting is more of a smokescreen to fool other characters into thinking that she is a ditsy old woman rather than an intelligent and shrewd judge of character who is listening to everything they say.

MAGGIE SEFTON'S KELLY FLYNN SERIES (the first book is titled *Knit One, Kill Two*) features an amateur detective who relocates to Colorado, where she joins a knitting group and solves mysteries.

THE NEEDLECRAFT SERIES BY MONICA FERRIS is set in a needlework shop and touches on many types of stitching, including crewel, needlepoint, and cross-stitch. Series sleuth Betsy Devonshire has solved knitting-related mysteries like *Sins and Needles*, in which the murder victim is stabbed with a knitting needle.

WHILE MY PRETTY ONE KNITS by ANNE CANADEO is the first in the BLACK SHEEP series of knitting mysteries. Focused on a knitting group called (you guessed it) the Black Sheep, the first book in the series sees the owner of the group's local yarn store framed for murder.

Another hapless victim meets his maker courtesy of a knitting needle in *HASTY RETREAT* BY KATE GALLISON, part of a series featuring Episcopal priest and amateur detective Mother Lavinia Grey.

SALLY GOLDENBAUM writes the SEASIDE KNITTERS series, with titles like *Angora Alibi* and *A Fatal Fleece*.

Crime-writing legend RUTH RENDELL opted for a set of circular needles for the murder weapon in her 1988 novel *THE VEILED ONE*; Inspector Wexford must investigate the death of a woman who was garroted in the middle of a shopping mall.

You've heard of the Montagues and the Capulets and the Hatfields and the McCoys, but did you know that a deadly family feud started in the late 1800s over sheep?

That's how some people tell the story of the Pleasant Valley War, a long-running feud between the Tewksbury and Graham families in Arizona. In the 1880s, both families moved to adjacent land in a remote valley in Arizona. Over time, the ranching families fought over issues like water rights, borders, and grazing rights. The Grahams were cattle ranchers, and tensions ran high when the Tewksbury family began herding sheep for the Dagg brothers—men who had their eye on the fertile valley land for sheep grazing. When the Tewksburys' sheep crossed over into the Pleasant Valley, the Grahams and other cattle ranchers went ballistic (literally). Sheep were killed, and a shepherd employed by the Tewksburys was murdered. The feud escalated, with shootouts, lynchings, and general mayhem lasting for a decade. The feud didn't end until most of the major players in both families were dead. Some historians suggest that sheep weren't the cause of the hostilities between the families but rather the last straw that caused pre-existing tensions to boil over into violence. Regardless of the precise cause of the conflict, the Pleasant Valley War, as it is often called, is known as one of the bloodiest chapters in the history of American ranching.

THE COLLECTIONS OF THE SMITHSONIAN INSTITUTE include photographs taken by Constance Stuart Larrabee, who traveled to South Africa in 1948 on assignment. While there, she visited the Kimberley Mines, the center of diamond mining in that province, capturing images of the miners knitting in their spare time. She noted on one photograph, *"Many of the miners like to knit colorful sweaters and caps for themselves when off duty. The one man is still wearing his underground helmet, which protects his head from falling stone, when underground."*

SOCK KNITTERS: DO NOT VOLUNTEER to knit socks for Brahim Takioullah of Morocco. Named the man with the largest feet in the world by Guiness World Records, Takioullah's left foot measures 15 inches, and his right 14.76 inches.

Sometime in the late 19th century, fur traders introduced to New Zealand a species of marsupial called the brushtail possum. The possum is a nocturnal animal with large pointy ears, a bushy tail, and sharp claws. It also happens to have an especially warm and soft coat. The traders, hoping to create a market for the possum's pelt, set the animals loose. However, the possum has no natural predators in New Zealand, and its population has grown at a staggering rate. Brushtail possum harbor a strain of the tuberculosis bacterium that infects cattle and deer; the possum also can cause catastrophic damage to forests and harm birds, insects, snails, and other native species. It's the fur of this destructive possum, and not the opposum found in North America, that is used to create the airy, warm yarns milled in New Zealand by Zealana and other yarn producers.

UNUSUAL DYESTUFFS

■ **cochineal:** derived from a scaly insect that lives on cacti in South America and Mexico, bright red

■ **tyrian purple:** secretion from the gland of a certain sea snail found in the eastern Mediterranean, reddish-purple

■ **letharia vulpine:** poisonous lichen found in North America and Europe, yellow

■ **mushrooms:** depending on the species, may produce blue, yellow, or green

■ **sepia:** derived from the ink of the cuttlefish, a marine animal related to octopus and squid, brown

■ **mauveine:** derived from coal tar, mauve/purple

■ **kermes:** extracted from dried, unlayed eggs of an insect found on a specific species of Mediterranean oak tree, red

We call knitted throws or blankets "afghans," but why?

According to the Oxford English Dictionary, the first use of the term *afghan* to refer to a blanket-like item was a reference by Thomas Carlyle in 1833 to an "Afghaun shawl." We know that by the end of the 19th century, *afghan* was in usage to refer to a knitted or crocheted blanket. Obviously there is a connection to the country of Afghanistan, which has a long history of textile production. Some speculate that because Afghani rugs and blankets often featured geometric motifs, vivid color combinations, and stripe patterns, knitted or crocheted throws that featured similar designs were named after Afghani rugs or blankets.

For many years, the unwritten rule when it comes to baby clothes has been pink for girls and blue for boys. But the "pink is for girls" tradition is of relatively recent vintage. In the 1800s, most children wore white (perhaps because white clothes are easy to bleach), and both boys and girls wore dresses (perhaps to make it easier to change diapers). In the early part of the last century, clothing retailers and manufacturers introduced the idea of specifying colors for each gender—except the rule was the reverse, advocating pink for boys and blue for girls. A 1918 trade publication explained the distinction: "[P]ink, being a more decided and stronger color, is more suitable for the boy, while blue, which is more delicate and dainty, is prettier for the girl." Midway through the 20th century, the color preference shifted, with pink being assigned to girls and blue to boys. In the 1970s, the women's movement triggered a trend toward unisex baby clothes, but gender-specific items returned sometime in the 1980s, perhaps as a result of more widespread prenatal testing. Once parents learned the gender of their expected baby, they gravitated toward clothing items marketed specifically to that gender.

Sharp-eyed fans of *ROWAN* magazine will recall two celebrities who modeled Rowan garments before they were household names. British actor Eddie Redmayne modeled Rowan Denim sweaters before winning a Best Actor Academy Award for his portrayal of Stephen Hawking in the movie *The Theory of Everything*, while supermodel Kate Moss was photographed wearing intarsia sweaters in Rowan's iconic "Swallows and Amazons" photo shoot before she graced the Paris runways.

➤ IS IT A **CROCHET NEEDLE** OR A **CROCHET HOOK**?
According to crochet expert NANCY NEHRING, there is a difference. Nehring distinguishes between a tool with an integrated handle, which she terms a *crochet hook*, and a tool made of a hook mounted to a separate handle (often made of a different material), which she calls a *crochet needle*.

If in doubt about the weight of a **skein of mystery yarn,** try passing two strands of the yarn through the holes of a needle gauge. When the strands pass comfortably through a hole, you've found the approximate needle size to use.

◆ A piece of yarn walks into a bar. When he tries to order a drink, the bartender says, "We don't serve your kind here." The piece of yarn is sitting on the curb feeling sorry for himself, when he suddenly has a brilliant idea. He ties himself into a knot and unravels his ends. He goes back into the bar and orders a drink. The bartender says, "Hey, I know you! You're that piece of yarn I just threw out of here!" "No," says the yarn. "I'm a frayed knot."

◆ A state trooper was patrolling the highway and saw a car weaving all over the road. He pulled up behind the car and flashed his lights. The car didn't stop, so he drove up beside it and motioned to the driver. The car still didn't stop. He put on his lights and siren and finally got the driver's attention. When he looked through the window, he saw that she was frantically knitting. He motioned again to the driver, and she rolled down the window. Red in the face, he leaned out and yelled, "Pull over! Pull over!" She yelled back, "No, it's a cardigan!"

Q: Why did the pig farmer give up knitting?

A: She didn't want to cast her purls before swine.

Q: Why did the sheep avoid going to bars?

A: She didn't want to be carded.

◆ Police are looking for a man they have labeled the Knitting Needle Man. He is stabbing his victims with a knitting needle. Police believe he is following some sort of pattern.

WHERE and WHEN
was knitting first invented?

GOOD QUESTION. It's difficult to ascertain the origins of knitting for a variety of reasons—because the fibers used to create long-ago yarns were biodegradable and unlikely to survive long periods in the ground, and also because common household items weren't considered important enough for deliberate preservation. We can only make educated guesses based on the few artifacts that have survived.

FOR A LONG TIME, HISTORIANS POINTED to fragments of socks found in Egypt and Peru dating from 300 BC to AD 300, opining that these were the earliest known examples of knitting. But history is always subject to revision, and experts in needlework concluded that these socks were actually made with a single-needle technique called *nålbinding*. (Without getting too technical, nålbinding uses a single needle with an eye instead of two eyeless needles; instead of using a continuous length of yarn, it uses cut lengths of yarn. Some nålbinding stitches look very much like knitted stitches; others have a more distinctive appearance.)

MOST HISTORIANS BELIEVE that the oldest surviving knitted articles are the so-called Coptic socks found in Egypt and dating from the period AD 1000 to 1300. Historians agree that these socks are knit rather than made by nålbinding; they feature beautiful and complex stranded stitch patterns knit in cotton. Given the elaborate stranded designs on these socks and how beautifully they are constructed, we might assume that knitting had been going on in this area for a while prior to the time when the surviving socks were made. Even the most skilled knitters take some time to progress from simple one-color work to elaborate colorwork, and there must have been a great deal of trial and error to discover the clever methods required to make a sock fit the oddly shaped human foot. So our best guess, based on what we know now, is that knitting developed sometime in the period before AD 1000 to 1300 in Egypt. ✳

> ### Shetland ring or wedding ring shawls
> are knit in beautiful lace patterns and in such fine wool that, as Shetland expert Sarah Don wrote, "although they can measure up to 6 feet square, they can with ease be pulled through a woman's wedding ring."

Silk fiber is said to come from "silkworms."

However, what we think of as silkworms aren't technically worms, but rather the larvae of a moth. A single larvae eats 40,000 times its own weight in tree leaves from birth to the time it pupates—that means it takes more than 25 mulberry trees to obtain about 3 kilograms of silk. A single larvae can produce over 16 feet of fiber in one minute; one single silk filament can extend over 4,300 feet. It takes about 2,000 to 3,000 larvae to make a pound of silk. It's estimated that the world produces 70 billion miles of silk filament per year, an amount equal to 300+ round trips to the sun.

Although we usually envision cable-knit sweaters *(also known as fisherman's sweaters, arans, or ganseys)* in undyed cream-colored wool, traditionally these sweaters were knit in darker colors, particularly navy and charcoal. It wasn't until the 1930s, when cable-knit sweaters were marketed to the United States, that the cream-colored wool became indelibly associated with fisherman's sweaters.

Archeological findings in the Caucasus region of Georgia show that prehistoric humans were spinning, dyeing, and knotting flax fibers to make cords that may have been used for tools, sewing clothing, or weaving baskets more than 30,000 years ago.

Yarn bowls are a handy and beautiful way to prevent your balls and skeins of yarn from rolling around the floor and/or tangling.

While the precise design differs from artisan to artisan, the most popular are thrown by potters and feature a hole or J-shaped slot that the working strand of yarn can be threaded through, while the ball of yarn sits in the middle of the bowl instead of dancing all over the floor (and torturing the cat). Frugal alternatives: plastic bags with a zipper closure, colanders, teapots, empty plastic containers such as soda bottles (pull the bottom off to insert the ball and run the working strand out the top), empty baby wipe boxes, a regular bowl with a binder clip attached (run the yarn through the metal handle of the clip), a net bag from produce, or an old knee-high stocking (if you are old enough to know what that is).

QUOTES ABOUT KNITTING
Literature

"'Why do you have a cigarette lighter in your glove compartment?'" her husband, Jack, asked her. "'I'm bored with knitting. I've taken up arson.'"
– AUDREY NIFFENEGGER,
HER FEARFUL SYMMETRY

"As soon as I could use my hands she taught me to knit, which has been a great amusement."
– JANE AUSTEN,
PERSUASION

"I knit the afternoon away. I knit reasons for Elijah to come back. I knit apologies for Emma. I knit angry knots and slipped stitches for every mistake I ever made, and I knit wet, swollen stitches that look awful. I knit the sun down."
– LAURIE HALSE ANDERSON,
WINTERGIRLS

"The truth was, knitting was the only skill he had learned during the war that he enjoyed. There was something soothing about watching stitch after stitch pass across the needles, something meditative about the process."
– JESSICA DAY GEORGE,
*PRINCESS OF
THE MIDNIGHT BALL*

"To watch her was curiously soothing. Every harassed businessman, he thought, should have a tank of tropical fish at one end of his office and a woman knitting at the other."
– RUTH RENDELL,
MURDER BEING ONCE DONE

"Sitting here with one's knitting, one just sees the facts."
– AGATHA CHRISTIE,
*THE BLOOD-STAINED
PAVEMENT*

"'Oh, there you are, Albus,' he said. 'You've been a very long time. Upset stomach?'
'No, I was merely reading the Muggle magazines,' said Dumbledore. 'I do so love knitting patterns.'"
– J.K. ROWLING,
*HARRY POTTER AND THE
HALF-BLOOD PRINCE*

"'Can you row?' the Sheep asked, handing her a pair of knitting-needles as she spoke.
'Yes, a little—but not on land—and not with needles—' Alice was beginning to say."
– LEWIS CARROLL, *THROUGH
THE LOOKING-GLASS*

 "Knitting is the saving of life." – VIRGINIA WOOLF

KNITTING ACCESSORIES AND TOOLS:
A PRIMER

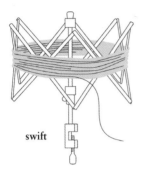

swift

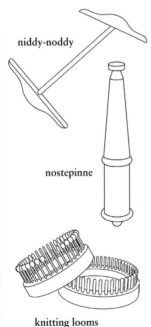

niddy-noddy

nostepinne

knitting looms

• **swift (umbrella swift):** a spoked device that clamps to a flat surface or comes with a stand. It has extendable arms to hold a hank of yarn. As the knitter winds the yarn, the arms rotate, allowing the yarn to feed freely with no handle or crank for turning the arms. Designed for knitters who need to turn hanks of yarn into balls.

• **skein winder:** a device with arms that allows a knitter to wind off hanks from a cone of yarn, or to rewind hanks to a different circumference. May be motorized or operated by hand. May contain a device for measuring yardage.

• **nostepinne:** of Scandinavian origin, it's said the word means "nest stick." It's a wooden hand tool used to create center-pull balls by winding the yarn at various angles around the stick.

• **lucet:** a flat tool with two prongs used to make knitted cord similar to I-cord.

• **niddy-noddy:** a tool that is used to wind hanks of yarn. It is shaped like a capital I, with one of the cross-bars turned at a 90-degree angle. An approximate measurement of length can be made by measuring the length of one wrap and multiplying by the total number of wraps.

• **lazy kate:** a device used to hold bobbins of yarn so that they feed easily for plying on a spinning wheel.

• **knitting loom:** a device with a series of pegs, either in a straight line (for flat knitting) or a circle (for knitting in the round). It allows the user to manipulate loops by hand or with a hook to create looped stitches.

• **Liaghra:** a Scottish tool similar to a swift; it consisted of two sticks crossed and set on a rotating pin in a block or base.

• **McMorran Yarn Balance:** a type of scale used to approximate the yardage per pound of a specific yarn. A piece of the yarn is placed on the balance. Small snips of the yarn are cut until the scale hits zero. The user then measures the length of the remaining piece of yarn and multiplies by 100 to find the estimated number of yards per pound of that yarn.

• **wooly board:** a device used to block sweaters that have been knit in the round. It consists of slats or dowels that form a rough sweater shape. Most allow for adjusting the dimensions at chest, length, neck, and perhaps shoulders/arms. ✳

According to traditions from the Canadian Navy in the Maritimes, sailors should wear knit wristers to protect against chafing but should never wear white gloves or mittens as they bring bad luck.

✳ ✳ ✳ ✳

It was said that if a woman knit a strand of her hair along with the yarn in the toe of a sock for her sailor-lover, he would always come back to her.

The Sheep Meadow, Central Park's only ballfield-free lawn, is filled with people nowadays, but many years ago it was filled with sheep. Frederick Law Olmsted and Calvert Vaux, the landscape architects who won the competition to design Central Park, originally included parade grounds for military drills. But the park's designers eventually decided that military use was not consistent with their vision of the park as a restful escape. So, from 1864 until 1934, pedigreed Southdown and Dorset sheep roamed the field instead, giving the Sheep Meadow its name. The sheep and shepherd lived nearby in a Victorian building, which later became the notable restaurant Tavern on the Green.

DESCRIPTION OF A 19TH-CENTURY SPINNING BEE

"Spinning bees and quilting bees were exclusively feminine industries. With each invitation to a spinning bee was sent a bunch of tow sufficient for two or three days' spinning, which the recipient was expected to turn into thread or yarn by or before the date fixed for the party. The acceptance of the [fiber] was equivalent to a formal acceptance of the invitation. On the appointed day each lady took her bunch of spun tow and proceeded early in the afternoon to the house of the hostess.
The afternoon was usually spent in the usually easy and unconventional manner that might be expected when a dozen or fifteen able bodied women of the neighborhood, who had not seen each other lately, are assembled. . . . The surest way for a lady to avoid being the subject of comment was to be at the meeting."
—*The Early Settlement of Dallas Twp., Luzerne Co., Pennsylvania* by Wm. Penn Ryman

---

Many historic and vintage patterns for handknit socks feature **vertical design elements called *clocks*** or, less frequently, *clox*. Knitting expert SEILA McGREGOR notes that early knitted socks copied design elements from the cloth hosiery that preceded them. She observed that vintage cloth stockings often featured embroidered designs decorating the ankle. These designs played an important structural role, too, by reinforcing the seams that they covered. Likewise, McGregor points out the frequent use of faux seams running down the back of vintage handknit hosiery. Socks knit in the round are by definition seamless, so the only purpose a back "seam" could serve is decorative.

The University of Glasgow appointed its ***first knitter in residence*** in the fall of 2014 to coincide with the university's Knitting in the Round project. The job description: "engaging members of the University (including students, support staff, and academics) with hand knit[ting]," with the precise duties to be determined during the residency. Susan McComb was lucky enough to be named to the position, surely a dream job for all those who work in wool.

SHEEP ANATOMY

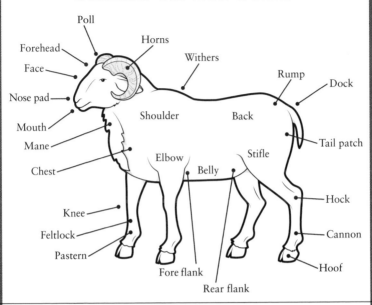

Poll
Horns
Forehead
Withers
Face
Rump
Dock
Nose pad
Shoulder
Back
Mouth
Mane
Tail patch
Chest
Elbow
Stifle
Belly
Knee
Hock
Feltlock
Cannon
Pastern
Hoof
Fore flank
Rear flank

SERICULTURE, the raising of silkworms in order produce silk, was begun in China around 2500 BC, when the emperor Huangdi directed his wife to look into the use of thread from the silkworm.

His wife (whose name is reported variously as Hsi Ling Shi, Lei Tsu, and Xi Ling Shi) figured out how to raise silkworms, wind off the silk, and use it for garments, earning her the honorific title "The Goddess of Silkworms." China remained the center of sericulture for centuries until countries like Japan and India broke the Chinese monopoly on the silk trade. Today, the top producers of silk are China, India, Uzbekistan, Brazil, Japan, North and South Korea, Thailand, Vietnam, and Iran. The top consumers of silk are the United States, Italy, Japan, India, France, China, the United Kingdom, Switzerland, Germany, United Arab Emirates, Korea, and Vietnam.

❖ ❖ ❖ ❖ ❖

ANGORA: *IS IT A TYPE OF RABBIT? OR A BREED OF GOAT?* **BOTH, ACTUALLY.**

The Angora is one of the oldest types of domestic rabbit, traditionally bred for its long, downy coat. There are several breeds of Angora rabbit, such as French Angora, Giant Angora, and Satin Angora. Angora rabbits produce very silky and fine wool (finer than cashmere), which is harvested from the rabbit by shearing, combing, or plucking. Depending on the precise breed, Angora rabbits can weigh up to 12 pounds or more. The name *angora* comes from the Turkish town of Ankara, known in the past as Angora. When you see yarn labeled as containing angora, the manufacturer is referring to the super-soft fur of the rabbit.

Just to make things confusing, there's also a breed of goat called Angora that produces long, silky hair and is also named after the Turkish city Angora/Ankara. Angora goats produce the fiber we call mohair—a long, lustrous fiber with a hint of a halo. Mohair is sheared from goats and often blended with other yarns and/or brushed to emphasize its halo.

Neither of the above should be confused with the Angora cat, a breed with—you guessed it—long, silky fur and named for the Turkish city. It was the Angora cat, rather than the goat or rabbit, that was so beloved by the James Bond villain Ernst Stavro Blofeld.

☛ Runners who knit, take note:

University of Missouri professor David Babcock set a new record on October 19, 2013, for longest scarf knitted while running a marathon. Babcock managed to create a 6-foot, 9-inch scarf as he ran, surpassing the prior record of 5 feet, 2 inches held by Britain's Susie Hewer.

POMPOMS: THOSE FLUFFY BALLS OF FIBER THAT OFTEN ADORN THE TOP OF A CAP.

According to the Merriam-Webster Dictionary, the word comes from the French *pompe*, meaning "tuft of ribbons," or the word *pompon*, meaning "an ornamental tuft or flower head." The uniform of the French navy features red pompoms on the top of the cap; pompoms are also commonly seen on tams, where they are sometimes called *toories*. Some Roman Catholic clergy wear hats called *birettas*, with four peaks and pompoms that signify rank based on color.

Manufacturers add all sorts of things to their products—vitamins, preservatives, colors, flavors—so why not add all sorts of things to yarn? Consider:

• **Hauk** yarn, by **Dale of Norway**, contained Teflon™ in order to enhance the yarn's water resistance.

• Several manufacturers have added scents to their yarn in recent years; **Lily Sugar-n-Cream,** for example, is offered in seven scents, including lavender, chamomile, and rose petal.

• **Red Heart Heart & Sole** sock yarn is treated with aloe vera, with the aim of softening the crafter's hands while making the yarn glide smoothly over needles and hooks.

• Do your feet sometimes feel too hot, sometimes too cold, but never just right? **Lorna's Laces Solemate** sock yarn uses Outlast™ technology to create a yarn that is designed with fibers that continuously interact with the body to moderate temperature.

• In 2012, **Zealana Yarns** of New Zealand produced a limited-edition yarn containing ground pearls in honor of the 30th anniversary of the reborn *Vogue Knitting.*

• Several manufacturers have added reflective fiber or thread to their yarns in order to make items reflect light at night, perfect for those who run, walk, or bike after sundown. **Schachenmayr Lumio** yarn is one; **Red Heart Reflective** is another.

If you're traveling in West Virginia, keep an eye out for the Sheepsquatch. Over the years, residents in West Virginia have reported seeing a white shaggy creature, about seven or eight feet tall, with horns like a ram. Dubbed "Sheepsquatch," the ovine-ish beast has drawn much attention—and skepticism—in the area. If you're one of the skeptics, then you probably don't want to hear about Maryland's Goatman . . .

☐ In England, an Act of Parliament dated 1677 made it a criminal offense to bury someone in a garment made of anything other than sheep's wool, whether *"made or mingled with Flax, Hempe, Silk, Haire, Gold, or Silver or in any Stuffe or thing other than what is made of Sheeps Wooll onely."* Ditto for coffin linings. Offenders were subject to a five-pound fine, which would be equivalent to more than $1,100 today.

⫸→ CRUEL AND UNUSUAL PUNISHMENT IN YARN SHOP NAMES

Gosh Yarn It *(Kingston, PA)*

Wooly Monmouth *(Monmouth, NJ)*

Darn Knit Anyway *(Stillwater, MN)*

ImagiKnit *(San Franscisco, CA)*

The Skein Attraction *(Teaneck, NJ)*

Cultured Purls *(Issaquah, WA)*

Ewe-Nique Yarns *(N. St. Paul, MN)*

Why Knot Knit *(Atlanta, GA)*

Ewetopia Fiber Shop *(Viroqua, WI)*

We'll Keep You In Stitches *(Chicago, IL)*

The Purly Gates *(Marietta, GA)*

Yarniverse *(Memphis, TN)*

Putting on the Knitz *(W. Newton, MA)*

Hissy Knit *(Los Angeles, CA)*

Communknity *(San Jose, CA)*

Knit and Caboodle *(St. Charles, MO)*

Yarnzilla *(Minnetonka, MN)*

Knit Happens *(Scottsdale, AZ & Oakleys, OH)*

Knit A Round Yarn Shop *(Ann Arbor, MI)*

Mad About Ewe *(Redding, CA)*

Have Ewe Any Wool *(Elmhurst, IL)*

Knitty Cat *(Centennial, CO)*

Knitter's Laine *(Shelburne, VT)*

Knotty Girl *(Fairfield, CT)*

Lettuce Knit *(Richmond, VA)*

Ewe'll Love It *(Nashua, NH)*

Ewe-Phoric Yarns *(Arnold, CA)*

Knot Another Hat *(Hood River, OR)*

Yarning for You *(San Marcos, CA)*

In November 1934, the *New York Times* reported that a group of 10 male students at Columbia University formed a knitting society they dubbed Knita-Nata-Nu. Dean Herbert Hawkes issued a brief statement of support: "I think that all students who want to should be allowed to knit. This is part of the liberty for which Columbia stands." The club was briefly the darling of the media, when photographers and reporters flocked to the Columbia bookstore to see the male knitters. However, the Columbia Spectator reported that the club was dissolved after a few days, but not before receiving a great deal of press and a card of yarn samples from The Garden Knitting Shop of Roxborough, Pennsylvania.

In the Middle Ages, the Cistercian order of monks were sometimes called "white monks," as they adopted clothing made from undyed or white wool.

Wool lovers

have no doubt seen the Woolmark logo—a licensed symbol adopted by a group of Australian woolgrowers to designate quality products made from wool.

Did you know:

▶ that the logo was created by an Italian designer, Francesco Saroglia, and selected as part of a competition from among dozens of entries?

▶ that the logo's design of four intertwined strands forming a skein is so timeless that it has never been altered or modernized?

▶ that in 2011, a top UK magazine in the field of visual communication voted the Woolmark logo the best logo of all time?

▶ that the logo can only appear on items made of 100 percent pure new wool that meets specific performance standards?

▶ that two derivative logos were introduced, the Woolmark Blend logo (for items consisting of 50 percent or more new wool, with only one other nonwool component subject to certain construction guidelines to

make testing feasible) and the Wool Blend logo (for items consisting of 30 to 49 percent new wool, with only one nonwool component in singles yarns)?

▶ that the Woolmark logo celebrated its 50th birthday in 2014?

❨ WHY DO WE COUNT SHEEP WHEN WE'RE TRYING TO SLEEP? Some believe the practice has its basis in the habit of medieval shepherds. Before going to sleep each night, shepherds who used communal pastures to graze their sheep employed a particular counting method before retiring for the night—hence the association between what was no doubt a repetitive, boring task and falling asleep. Other authorities have pointed to earlier references suggesting that some Islamic cultures connected counting sheep with sleeping. An Oxford University study showed, however, that no matter what the source, visualizing a relaxing scene from nature, like a beach, is a superior method of relaxing at bedtime rather than imagining sheep cavorting over a fence.

It is said that US President James Buchanan liked to *crochet in his spare time.*

If you have trouble remembering the difference between **s2kp** and **sk2p**, or don't understand why a yarn over is sometimes called "yarn round needle," consider yourself lucky that you weren't knitting 200 years ago.

⠀➤ We take for granted the amount of standardization that has developed in knitting terminology and pattern writing, but back then, each author used her own set of terms, and often not even consistently within the same book. A yarn over, for example, could be called loop stitch, widening, a cast over, an increase, bringing the thread forward, or turning over. Purl stitches might be called "pearl" stitches, seamed stitches, working a back row, or a stitch with the yarn in the front. A decrease might be indicated by telling the knitter to narrow, lessen, or reduce; some instructions defined the precise method of decreasing (knitting two stitches together was common) while others did not. Ditto for increases, which were sometimes indicated by telling the knitter to widen, raise, or make 1. Some but not all patterns were written using abbreviations as a shorthand for stitches. The abbreviations were also not standardized and differed from author to author. By today's standards, these abbreviations seem particularly hard to fathom. For example, in one of JANE GAUGAIN's knitting manuals, the abbreviation "P" stands for a knit stitch (representing "plain" stitch) while "B" represented a purl stitch (representing a "back" stitch or row).

In the Middle Ages, a homespun cloth called *wadmal* was a vital part of the northern European economy. The Icelandic currency was based on wadmal, and prices were calculated in units of cloth called ells. In the Shetland Islands, wadmal was used by residents to pay their taxes and rents; in fact, the first detailed written records of Shetland rents and taxes show that payments were made mainly in wadmal. Denominations of the cloth included the cuttell, which was a piece of cloth about 2 feet long; a shilling, equal to 6 cuttells; and packs, consisting of 60 ells each.

UNUSUAL YARN NAMES

- Soft Hair *(Pingouin)*
- Twice Nice *(Mary Maxim)*
- Fuzzy Wuzzy *(Patons)*
- OoLaLa *(Reynolds)*
- Fatigues *(Trendsetter Yarns)*
- Saxatones *(Bear Brand)*
- Glimmerfluff *(Columbia-Minerva)*
- Sugar Rush *(Queensland)*
- Linie 124 Gaucho *(ONline)*
- Landlord *(Schoeller+Stahl)*
- Southern Comfort *(Twilleys of Stamford)*
- Punk *(Schoeller-Stahl)*
- Soap *(Artful Yarns)*
- Turtle *(Adriafil)*
- Smaragd *(Austermann)*
- Hip Hop *(Berroco)*
- No Smoking *(Filatura di Crosa)*
- Fanny *(Katia)*
- Flotsam *(Louisa Harding)*
- Cocktail *(Austermann)*
- Funky Zebra *(Cleckheaton)*
- Linie 76 Cup *(ONline)*
- Boogie *(Schoeller+Stahl)*
- Mellosheen *(Columbia-Minerva)*
- Great Lake High Trek *(Mary Maxim)*
- Stupendo *(Trendsetter Yarns)*
- Blarney-Spun *(Bernat)*
- Scamper *(Columbia-Minerva)*

IN THE EARLY 1960S, A NEW WARDEN AT THE INFAMOUS FEDERAL PRISON ALCATRAZ GAVE INMATES THE CHANCE TO EARN SPECIAL PRIVILEGES: they could purchase 4-inch-long crochet hooks or thin plastic knitting needles, yarn, patterns, and instruction books. Inmates were not allowed to keep the items they made. As noted in *Escape from Alcatraz* by J. Campbell Bruce, "Knitting needles flashed in fingers that once knew only triggers as the erstwhile bank robbers purled one, seldom dropped two, and skeins of yarn sped wondrously into sweaters." In fact, the warden was so taken with the mens' work that he displayed several doilies they created in his office. ～

Richard Arkwright, inventor of the spinning frame technology and a leading figure in Britain's industrial revolution, made his living for a time by buying and selling human hair used for the manufacture of wigs.

The first American manufacturer of crochet hooks and knitting needles was the Boye Company, founded in 1906 by James Boye along with two men from the sewing machine industry. In 1913, Boye introduced the first complete line of crochet hooks made in America.

Have you ever drunk from a knitting cup?

Seventeenth-century playwright and poet Ben Jonson refers to securing "a knitting cup" in his comedy *The Magnetic Lady*. Shortly after some medieval wedding ceremonies, a cup of wine was passed around and all who assisted in the wedding drank from it. (Shakespeare calls it the "contracting cup" in *The Winter's Tale*.)

Can't find a stitch marker?

Knitters have used all of the following in a pinch: *bobby pins,* safety pins, thin slices of a *plastic drinking straw,* paper clips, *twist ties,* small hair ties, *rubber bands, spare earrings,* loops of yarn, and *embroidery floss.*

⫸→ MEASUREMENTS OF
COMMON TERMS

Need to measure your knitted work but don't have a ruler or tape measure with you? Approximate the size of your knitting by using these common standard measurements based on easily found items.

Standard business card: 3½ in. x 2 in.

Standard credit card: 3⅜ in. x 2⅛ in.

US dollar bill: 6⅙ in. x 2½ in.

Canadian dollar bill: 6 in. x 2¾ in.

Letter-sized paper: 8½ in. x 11 in.

CD case: 5 in. x 5½ in.

Small index card: 3 in. x 5 in.

☛ *A sheep named Deveronvale Perfection sold for £231,000 (about $350,520.80 as of mid-2015) in 2009, shattering previous records. Why such a staggering sum?* The lamb was a top specimen in its breed—the Texel breed, popular for its meat—and its owner could expect to earn back his investment, and then some, by selling the sheep's semen to breeders around the world.

A sheep that can pay its way for its breeder is one thing, but another breed of sheep, called the Dolan sheep, is reportedly drawing even higher prices among the wealthy in China. Dolan sheep are extremely rare—some breeders estimate that there are only about a thousand Dolan sheep alive today. They have unusually curved noses, long floppy ears, and a double tail; Dolans with a dark coat and white tail are particularly prized. One breeder in Kashgar, China, was reportedly offered more than one million dollars for a six-year-old Dolan ram, but he refused to sell.

If, however, you are looking for a more economical way to go, rest assured that you can purchase a purebred sheep of a less exotic breed for roughly $200 to $500 in the United States. Sheep without documented lineage cost even less.

AN OLD CORNISH LEGEND IS ALSO A
CAUTIONARY TALE FOR THOSE WHO WOULD SHIRK
THEIR KNITTING AND SPINNING DUTIES.
The old tale "Duffy and the Devil" tells of a maiden who is scolded and beaten by her stepmother for abandoning her fiber work in order to chase boys. A squire sees the maiden being punished and offers to let her come live with him. The maiden agrees—only to be put to work knitting and spinning by the squire's housekeeper. She curses the spinning wheel, and the devil appears, offering to do her work for three years, after which she will become his unless she can guess his name. The three years pass quickly, and the maiden has no idea what the devil's true name is. As the deadline nears, she starts to mope, and the squire, trying to cheer her up, tells her about the funny man he saw in the forest, chanting, *"Duffy, you'll never know that my name is Terrytop, Terrytop, Terrytop!"* The maiden correctly guesses that the devil she summoned is the same funny man and sends the devil packing. In 1974, the tale was turned into a Caldecott Medal-winning children's book entitled *Duffy and the Devil.*

UNUSUAL, **WEIRD**, AND/OR *WONDERFUL* THINGS PEOPLE HAVE KNIT

1. Overalls

2. Apple cozies
(Yes, knitted covers for apples. Like the fruit.)

3. Knitted versions of a dissected frog, fetal pig, and rat

4. Cheese grater

5. Knitted model of DNA

6. Squid

7. Models of the digestive and female reproductive systems

8. Beets

9. Extension cord

10. Dalek (from the television show *Dr. Who*)

11. Candy-corn-shaped pastries

12. Wedding cakes

13. Light switch plate cover

14. Toaster cover

15. Guinea pig sweater

16. Reusable mop cover

17. Viking beard/hat combo

18. Sweater with periodic table of elements

19. Elvis wig

Felting vs. fulling: what's the difference?

Technically speaking, felting is a process of condensing and matting fibers together to form a thick cloth. Wet felting involves using hot, soapy water and agitation on layers of fibers until they mesh together. Needle felting achieves the same result without water by use of a sharp needle to tangle and compress the wool. The process that most knitters use is, strictly speaking, called *fulling*. The knitter uses already-spun fiber to knit an object, usually at a much looser gauge and at dimensions that are much larger than the desired finished size. The object is then submerged into warm, soapy water and agitated, either by hand or by a washing machine, to produce the fabric we call felt.

THE MEDIEVAL KNITTING GUILDS OF EUROPE allowed only men to become members—although it is reported that in some guilds, if a member died, his wife was allowed to take his place.

Today's crafters don't think twice about how easy it is to tell the size of a knitting needle or crochet hook. But those handy needle gauges that so many knitters and crocheters keep in their bags weren't invented until sometime in the first half of the 19th century.

In the early 1840s, knitting author FRANCES LAMBERT announced in *My Knitting Book* that she had invented what she called a *filière* to measure different sizes of knitting needles and crochet hooks. Her book *The Hand-Book of Needlework* (1842) provided illustrations of Lambert's Standard Filière, made of ivory, as well as a regular industrial wire gauge used for a process called wire drawing, where wire is pulled through a die. Lambert's gauge contained holes numbered from 1 to 26, which she asserted were sized to match standard industrial gauges. Other knitting writers of the time, including CORNELIA MEE and ELIZABETH JACKSON, produced and sold their own gauges, though there were discrepancies among the sizes of various gauges. Some knitting gauges from the 1800s were made with notches, rather than holes, for measuring needle diameter, while still others contained long slots of graduating sizes. Gauges were made in many shapes. Rectangular and circular ones were common, while other gauges took the form of crescents, triangles, bells, diamonds, and even items such as a cornucopia, a set of airplane propellers, and a beehive. Early gauges were made of metal, wood, and bone. Then, in the 20th century, celluloid, plastic, Bakelite, and pressed cardboard were used. Perhaps even more delightful than the gauges themselves were some of the proprietary names given to them: the Wheel of Fortune Knitting Pin Gauge, the Cornucopia gauge, the Griffin gauge (with an etching of a griffin in the middle), the Clive, the Aero, the Fairfax, the Peacock, the Jesco Knit-Gyde, and the Reel Tidi. ✳

Bell shape gauge, circa 1800 ☛

37

⫸→ CHARLES DICKENS created the infamous Madame Defarge, who knitted messages into her stitchwork in *A Tale of Two Cities*. Dickens's vivid character was based, in part, on the real-life tricoteuses of the French Revolution—supporters of the Revolution who would sit near the guillotines and knit while watching executions, or who brought their knitting into meetings of the Revolutionary assemblies.

IT WASN'T A STRETCH FOR DICKENS to take the idea of a tricoteuse and run with it, emphasizing Mme. Defarge's bloodlust and thirst for revenge against the aristocracy. Indeed, the notion of women sitting placidly with their knitting while decapitated heads plop into baskets sounds horrifying. (Even more horrifying is the notion of said women cheering on the executions while, say, turning a heel without missing a stitch.) When the stereotype of knitting is the kindly grandmother with fluffy wool making sweaters for her grandchildren, well, a figure like Mme. Defarge stands out in our mind as particularly unnatural.

BUT CONSIDER THE ROLE AND STATUS OF WOMEN in France at this time. In the early days of the Revolution, women were permitted to play a more active role. In October 1789, women led a march on Versailles, protesting the high price and scarcity of bread to much revolutionary acclaim. One historian notes that women were permitted to attend meetings, meet in their own groups, and play an active role in street politics. By the end of 1793, they were prohibited from meeting in political groups, were denied the right to speak at the General Assembly, and were told that the Revolution did not need their activism. Small wonder that the tricoteuses chose to sit and watch executions take place, taking a passive but public role after being deprived of an official role in the Revolution. ✳

In *A Treasury of Knitting Stitches,* her first stitch collection, BARBARA G. WALKER includes a stitch called King Charles Brocade. The stitch pattern is said to be based on the damask, or brocade-like, pattern of a knitted waistcoat or shirt worn by King Charles I at his execution in 1649. The garment was knit of very fine silk in a light blue color, with a small collar and button-up neck, and it is now part of the collection of the Museum of the Tower of London. The shirt has been tested twice to confirm whether stains that appear on it are in fact blood, but testing was inconclusive. However, testing did show that the stains were from some bodily fluid.

➤ The next time you attend a rodeo, keep an eye out for the **mutton busting event.** Sometimes called wool riding, the event features children trying to ride a sheep in the ring for as long as they can, à la bull riding. Children between the ages of four and seven can enter if they weigh less than 60 pounds. Mutton busting events are extremely popular, sometimes attracting hundreds of kiddie riders. Don't worry, parents—the little mutton busters wear helmets and other protective gear.

WILL A SHEEP'S WOOL GROW FOREVER? It depends on the kind of sheep. Primitive or wild sheep breeds, like the Bighorn Sheep in Wyoming and the Soay, which live on a small island off the coast of Scotland, still shed, or "molt," their coat each year. But the fleece of domesticated breeds, like the Merino, will continue to grow as long as the sheep is alive—even though lack of shearing can lead to health issues, such as perishing from summer heat due to an excessively thick wool coat.

Is there a difference between lace knitting and knitted lace? Experts agree that in lace knitting, the eyelet patterns and accompanying decreases are worked only on right-side rows—the wrong-side rows are either all knit or all purled. In knitted lace, the eyelet patterns and decreases are worked on every row. You'll find, however, that the terms are used by many knitters without regard for the distinction.

As far back as the 1500s, crochet was once called *nun's work* or *nun's lace.*

YEAR OF DESIGNATIONS
FOR THE YARN LOVER

JANUARY	FEBRUARY	MARCH
NATIONAL HOBBY MONTH	(first Thursday) NATIONAL SWEATER DAY (Canada)	NATIONAL CRAFT MONTH • NATIONAL CROCHET MONTH • **MARCH 20** NATIONAL SWEATER DAY (US)

APRIL 3	MAY 3	JUNE
NATIONAL TWEED DAY	NATIONAL LOST SOCK MEMORIAL DAY	(second Saturday) WORLD WIDE KNIT IN PUBLIC DAY

JULY 2	OCTOBER	NOVEMBER
WORLD UFO DAY (okay, it's for extraterrestrials, but how about dragging out an unfinished project?)	(first full week) NATIONAL SPINNING AND WEAVING WEEK • (third Saturday) I LOVE YARN DAY	NATIONAL KNIT A SWEATER MONTH

In 1919, knitter **JANET BOWIE,** a resident of Otago, New Zealand, was named a Member of the Most Excellent Order of the British Empire in recognition of her service to the war effort: Bowie knitted **736 pairs of socks** for World War I soldiers.

It takes about **1 pound** of mohair fiber to make a lightweight sweater and about **¼ pound** to make a good-sized scarf.

So often when we try to determine the history of a knitting tradition, we cannot determine exactly where and when this specific tradition began—which makes it all the more satisfying when a folk knitting tradition can be traced all the way back to a specific knitter.
Such is the case with Selbu knitting.

When we think of Norwegian knitting, we envision mittens and sweaters knit in two colors (often black and white or red and white), with snowflakes, small geometric patterns, and larger motifs like flowers and reindeer. This distinctive style of knitting originated in the Selbu district of Norway and can be traced back to a knitter named Marit Emstad, who worked for a farmer in the 1850s. The farmer received a pair of stockings knitted with a simple two-color pattern as a Christmas present from another one of his workers. He admired the effect and asked Marit if she could knit something similar. Marit could. She produced a pair of mittens with black-and-white stars based on an embroidery pattern she had seen. Soon knitters all over Selbu were experimenting with intricate two-color patterns, primarily for knitted mittens and gloves.

As is often the case, declining economic prospects in the Selbu region led residents to rely on selling their knitted goods to bring in additional income. In the early part of the 20th century, Selbu-style mittens became all the rage in Oslo; the popularity of the mittens was probably helped when the sport of skiing became popular. More and more residents turned to knitting as a way to supplement their incomes, seeking to benefit from the demand. Unfortunately, over time, the quality of some of the knitted goods deteriorated. Concerned about protecting the reputation and "brand" of Selbu knitting, local shopkeepers set up the Selbu Handiwork Cooperative in 1934. The cooperative standardized patterns and monitored the quality of Selbu-knitted goods. ✳

To My Much Esteemed President Abraham Lincoln

Dear Sir:

Please allow an auld Lady of ninty one years of age to present to you a very humble testimony of esteem & confidence in the shape of a pair of socks knit with my own hands & allow me to say that I remember the trials passed through in revolution days. I lost to Brothers out of three that was in the servis of the country, besides Uncles & a number of cousins & my prayer to Him that doethe all things well, that holds the this [sic] nation in the hollow of his hand & hath continued my life to this time, & has enabled me to work almost dailey from the commencement of this rebellion to the present hour for the soldiers (God bless them) that you might be richly indowed with that wisdom which you have so much knowledge to enable you to beare so great responsibilities & to do that that is for the good of our bleeding Country & I do pray that you may live to see this rebellion ended & with it slavery (which I do abominate) wiped from our land, & long there after to witness & enjoy the fruits of your labour—you will pardon this intrusion upon your time & believe me to be your friend & friend of my bleeding country;

Sarah Phelps
Groton, N.H. Jan 7. 1865.

Clothing was made without pockets

during the Middle Ages, so people used small purses to carry some of the things they needed—rosary beads, say, or a small prayer book. Small bags called relic purses were knitted in order to store bones and other items used to commemorate the lives of saints.

In early 2015, the Craft Yarn Council
expanded its Standard Yarn Weight Chart to include
an eighth category called

Jumbo Yarn.

Creation of super-thick yarns for the trend in arm knitting
required the change; the new yarns were so thick that they needed
their own category for greater accuracy.

USES FOR LEFTOVER YARN
If your knitting mojo is knackered and your crochet creativity has crashed, here are some alternatives for using up those bits and bobs of leftover yarn:

➤ Use yarn to wind around popsicle sticks to create a God's eye.

➤ Shellac a partial ball of yarn (crochet thread works well) and turn it into a vase.

➤ Make pompoms and use to adorn a wreath or bunting.

➤ Wrap it: colorful strands can go around a wreath form, a piece of cardstock to create a bookmark, prefab wooded initials, vases, or a gift wrapped in plain paper. Or how about wrapping lampshades, bangles, or photo frames? The sky's the limit.

➤ Braid yarn and use for a giant cowl or belt, or sew braids together to make a rug.

➤ Use yarn leftovers for cross-stitch, needlepoint, or embroidery.

➤ Create eggs or festive decorations by wrapping yarn coated in laundry starch around balloons; when dry, pop the balloons.

➤ Make tassels and use to adorn a necklace, or mix with pompoms for a cute mobile.

➤ A small loom will turn odd balls of yarn into scarves.

In ancient Latvian tradition, mittens were often given as gifts.
A bride would present mittens to members of her husband's family
at the wedding, and mittens were given at funerals to those who dug
the grave and otherwise participated in the ceremony.

KNITTING ACRONYMS FROM THE KNITLIST

The KnitList, a message board hosted by Yahoo Groups, was founded on September 2, 2000, and, as of this writing, has 9,210 members. Run by moderators called "list moms," the number of KnitList posts peaked in January 2005, when more than 3,200 posts were created by members in a single month. The KnitList has helped to popularize a unique blend of acronyms and slang terms that Internet-savvy knitters continue to use, such as

- **tink:** a verb meaning to ravel out knitting stitch by individual stitch. Tink is *knit* spelled backward.

- **FO:** finished object; a knitting project finally completed

- **frog:** a verb meaning to rip out knitting a row at a time, or as the frog says, "Rip it!"; also used as part of *frog pond*, a pile of unfinished items awaiting raveling

- **EZ:** Elizabeth Zimmermann

- **SABLE:** stash acquisition beyond life expectancy; refers to the accumulation of yarn that one hasn't knit yet

- **OTN:** on the needles; a project in process

- **UFO:** unfinished object; also known as WIP, or work in progress

- **TOAD:** trashed object abandoned in disgust

- **KIP:** knitting in public

- **second sock syndrome:** tendency of sock knitters to complete the first sock in a pair but not the second

- **KAL or CAL:** knit- or crochet-along

- **AKC or OKC:** actual or obligatory knitting content; used when a knitting forum requires a post to contain at least a token statement about knitting, even if a pretext for what the poster really wants to say

☛ THE WORLD'S FIRST SOCCER MATCH PLAYED BY SHEEP WAS HELD IN JUNE 2014 IN NOBSA, COLOMBIA, when Andean artisans arranged a "game" between two teams of 10 sheep each. One team was dressed in Colombia's national colors, and the other in Brazil's. Shepherds spent two weeks training the sheep to kick foam balls through a wooden goalpost. While the big game was less than stellar from a sports standpoint—tenders had to keep tugging at the sheep's leads to prevent them from clumping together in a flock and eating the grass—the final score was 4–3 in Colombia's favor.

What do Navajo weaving, Amish quilts, and Persian rugs have in common?

All are handcrafts associated, rightly or wrongly, with the idea of the deliberate mistake. It's commonly said that Navajo weavers, Amish quilters, and Persian rug makers intentionally insert a mistake in their work in order to avoid the sin of pride: only the deity can achieve perfection, these stories claim, and humans should not be arrogant enough to believe that they, too, can achieve perfection. Like many bits of folklore that sound believable, though, it's difficult to find historical confirmation that the deliberate mistake was an actual belief of the crafters instead of marketing spin. For example, search the phrase "humility block," and numerous hits tell of this tradition as being usually associated with the Amish. Several noted quilt historians sought in vain to find confirmation that the Amish subscribed to this belief, however, and eventually concluded that the humility block was a way for observers to explain why a talented quilter might miss a few stitches, leave a block or motif at a wonky angle, or use a fabric that seemed to clash. Some have even questioned the logic behind the notion, wondering whether it is in fact more arrogant to believe that one's work is so good that there will be no mistakes other than one deliberately added. Whether the deliberate mistake is a long-standing belief of crafters or a more modern way to explain mistakes, it does have the advantage of easing the disappointment a crafter may feel when she notices a mistake long after the project is finished.

KNITTING MACHINES CAN CREATE STITCHES using rows of needles working back and forth or in the round like a hand knitter, but engineers have yet to come up with A MACHINE THAT CAN EXACTLY REPLICATE HAND CROCHET made by a hook. While some machines are able to mimic crochet stitches, they use rows of needles rather than a hook and are sometimes called crochet knitting machines or warp crochet machines.

A SELECTION OF ARTWORK
FEATURING FIBER ARTS

■ KNITTING

William-Adolphe Bouguereau
The Knitting Girl 1869
• Oil

Winslow Homer
Mending the Nets 1882
• Watercolor/gouache

Bertram von Minden
Knitting Madonna 1400–1410
• Tempera

Jean-François Millet
The Knitting Lesson 1869
• Oil

Beatrix Potter
Josephine Rabbit Knitting 1904
• Watercolor

Thomas Eakins
Study of a Woman Knitting
Date Unknown
• Oil

Mary Cassatt
The Young Bride 1875
• Oil

Frida Kahlo
*Portrait of Doña
Rosita Morillo* 1944
• Oil

Grace Coddington Smith
The Sox Knitter 1914
• Oil

■ CROCHET

Mary Cassatt
*Lydia Crocheting in the
Garden at Marly* 1880
• Oil

Edmund Tarbell
Girl Crocheting 1904
• Oil

Edward Thompson Davis
The Crochet Lesson 1850
• Oil

■ SPINNING

Max Liebermann
The Flax Barn at Laren 1887
• Oil

Eleuterio Pagliano
A Spinner 1869
• Oil

Gustave Courbet
*La Fileuse Endormie
(The Sleeping Spinner)* 1853
• Oil

Friedrich Ortlieb
At the Spinning Wheel
Date Unknown
• Oil

■ WINDING

Frederic Lord Leighton
Winding the Skein 1878
• Oil

RAYON
You've seen it on yarn and clothing labels, but what is it?

☞ Originally known as "artificial silk," rayon is an artificially created fiber from a natural source—cellulose, found in the cells of green plants. The story of rayon goes back to the 19th century, when scientists were attempting to create a cheaper alternative to silk. The first patent for artificial silk was issued in 1855 to Swiss chemist Georges Audemars. Audemars used a mixture containing bark from a mulberry tree to create threads, but the process was too slow to be used for commercial production. When the silk industry in France was threatened by a disease affecting silkworms, a French nobleman named Hilare de Chardonnet began experimenting with ways to turn cellulose into usable fiber. In 1884, Chardonnet was granted a patent for a process whereby he extruded a cellulose solution through small glass tubes. In 1889, after working to decrease the flammability of the fiber, he presented rayon to the public at the Paris Exposition; the next year, he opened a factory to produce *la soie de Chardonnet*, or Chardonnet silk.

The rayon industry took off, and in 1925 the US Federal Trade Commission gave artificial silk the name *rayon*. Originally the term *rayon* applied to all fibers derived from cellulose, but in 1952, the FTC divided cellulose-derived fibers into two categories: rayon (made from pure cellulose) and acetate (made from a cellulose compound). Major sources for making rayon are trees—hemlock, spruce, and pine trees, to be precise.

JAMES H. BOYE,
cofounder of the needle company that bears his name, was a **prolific inventor.**
Among the patents he registered are a can opener, safety pin, needle threader, key holder, penknife, combination thimble and needle holder, pencil sharpener, barn door hasp, nutmeg grater, and golf club.

Contributors to the nonprofit group The Ships Project have donated 257,400 knitted and crocheted hats and 314,600 "cool ties" (sewn neckties with water-absorbing crystals) for American soldiers stationed abroad.

Number of CALORIES BURNED per hour by KNITTING :

102

Activities that use FEWER CALORIES per hour than KNITTING:

listening to music	74
meditating	57
watching television	89
kissing	72
sleeping	57

SOME COUNTRIES WHERE SHEEP OUTNUMBER PEOPLE

Also known as highest density rate of sheep per capita, or high sheep to peeps ratio:

- Falkland Islands (166:1)
- New Zealand (7+:1)
- Mongolia (nearly 7:1)
- Australia (just under 4:1)
- Iceland (3:1)
- Uruguay (approx. 2.5:1)
- Turkmenistan (1.5:1)

⟫→ THE ORDER OF THE GOLDEN FLEECE

is a chivalrous society created by Philip III (Philip the Good) in 1430 to celebrate his marriage to Isabella of Portugal. Originally, the order had one grand master and 23 knights, but was later expanded to include 31 and then 51 knights. The purposes of the society were to uphold the ideals of chivalry, defend the Catholic faith, and to promote the interests of the dukes of Burgundy. The badge of the order consisted of a golden sheepskin suspended from a jeweled collar; variations in the style and materials used to make the insignia developed over time. It is said that the sheepskin symbolized the great wealth that Philip had achieved due to the wool trade.

Hemp Happiness

■ The flag that Betsy Ross sewed was made of 100 percent hemp fabric.

■ Levi's blue jeans were originally made from hemp.

■ George Washington and Thomas Jefferson grew hemp on their plantations.

■ The first Gutenburg Bibles were made of hemp.

■ Henry Ford experimented with hemp while trying to build cars from farm products, and his first Model-T ran on hemp fuel.

■ It was legal to pay one's taxes with hemp in the United States from 1631 until the beginning of the 19th century.

■ Eminent painters such as Rembrandt and Van Gogh painted on hemp canvas.

■ Many yarn companies have used hemp to create strong, durable, breathable yarns, such as Elsebeth Lavold Hempathy, Lanaknits AllHemp and Hempwol, and Martha Stewart Crafts Cotton-Hemp Yarn.

The *taatit*

is a type of woolen rug that has been woven and knotted on the Shetland Isles for centuries. Early examples of the taatit date from the 1760s, although the rugs stopped being made in any significant quantity in the mid-20th century. Taatits were made in a two-step process. First, a background fabric was woven in a plain weave using thick wool. Second, pieces of thinner wool yarn (2-ply wool) were sewn onto the background fabric using a needle with a large eye. By looping the yarn around two strands of wool in the background fabric, a pile about ½ inch long was created. Taatits were made in two halves that were then sewn together and bordered with a simple hem. Geometric, floral, or abstract motifs were often used, with the most frequently used colors including natural white, natural brown, blue, purplish pinks, and orange-reds. Historically, the rugs were used as bedcovers in Shetland, mainly by rural families.

{ **A crafting get-together** has been known, at various times, as a knitting bee, *a knitting sitting*, a frolic, *a stitch-n-bitch*, a knit-in, and *a knitting circle*. }

MOM RINKER

IF YOU TAKE A WALK ALONG THE WISSAHICKON CREEK IN PHILADELPHIA, YOU'LL COME ACROSS A ROCK CALLED MOM RINKER'S ROCK. The rock memorializes an innkeeper named Molly "Mom" Rinker, who frequently served British soldiers food and ale. Rinker spent so much time around the Redcoats that she began listening to their conversations, picking up tidbits of information and writing them on slips of paper. Mom Rinker would then head out to her favorite knitting place—a rock by a cliff—where she would make socks and other items for the rebel troops. When she had a piece of intelligence, she would carefully wrap yarn around the slips of paper and lower the resulting ball off the cliff, where a waiting soldier would grab the ball of yarn and take the papers to George Washington. Although it's hard to know exactly how much of the legend of Mom Rinker is true, General John Armstrong credited Rinker's intelligence-gathering with saving his men, stating, "I remain convinced that without this brave woman surely we of 300 men strong were doomed that day."

In 1995, the Regia company in Germany originated a novel printing technique called *Ringel* that allowed the knitter to create circular stripes without changing yarns—the colors were dyed in the sock yarn. Later, Regia developed more complex self-patterning yarn, including jacquard and Fair Isle patterning. Other companies also began producing competing lines of self-patterning sock yarn, leading to the plethora of choices—stripes, swirls, zigzags, even American flag patterning—that today's sock knitter enjoys.

The cover model on *Vogue Knitting* magazine has most often been a brunette—47% of the time, according to an unscientific review. Blondes came in second place, with about 38.8% of VK covers. Just under 1% of covers featured redheads. And only one cover (less than 1 percent) featured a gray-haired model—the talented and handsome designer Kaffe Fassett. (For statisticians wondering why the total is less than 100 percent: the remaining covers featured models with hats or hoods obscuring their hair color.)

Sick of getting chilly fingers when you take off your gloves to use the touchscreen on your smartphone or tablet?

The next time you knit yourself a pair of gloves, use conductive thread as a carry-along when knitting the tip of the index fingers and/or thumbs. Conductive thread is sold by various Internet suppliers and is usually made of stainless steel or silver—the metal is what makes the thread conductive.

IN SOME BREEDS OF SHEEP, LIKE SHETLAND AND SOAY, the sheep's wool stops growing in late spring. Weeks later, the wool begins to naturally separate from the animal. The wool can then be plucked from the sheep in a process called *rooing*. (Fear not: it doesn't hurt the sheep when the wool is plucked.) Some individual sheep and some family lines have wool more susceptible to rooing, while some sheep will shed only part of their fleece so that the remainder must be clipped by hand.

Knitting expert MARY THOMAS opines that the "tail" that often appears at the top of a beret or fez is a remant from the original knitting process.

Thomas says that when a beret or fez is knit, the crafter leaves the tail as a reminder of how it was made, marking the last stitches that the knitter worked. After felting, the individual stitches meld together but the tail remains, serving a decorative and symbolic purpose.

The oldest continuously operating yarn shop in the United States IS HEINDSELMAN'S, LOCATED IN

PROVO, UTAH. The shop first began doing business in 1904 in a corner of a drugstore, where George "Doc" Heindselman made eyeglasses for local residents. The shop later moved, and Doc's wife began stocking yarn and embroidery supplies. Today the grandson of the founders owns and operates the shop, which also features gift items as well as supplies for other crafts such as needlepoint and embroidery.

CELEBRITY KNITTERS
Political / Historical

Eleanor Roosevelt
•
Susan B. Anthony
•
Grace Coolidge
•
Madeleine Albright
•
Edith Roosevelt
•
Australian Prime Minister
Julia Gillard
•
Sojourner Truth
•
Queen Victoria
•
Dionne quintuplets
•
Tsarina Alexandra
Feodorovna of Russia
•
Monica Lewinsky

One day in the 1960s, a woman named Lorraine Linstead wanted to knit a baby afghan but only had straight needles that wouldn't be long enough to hold all the stitches. Always frugal, she asked her husband, Robert, an engineer and tinkerer, if he could create one long, connected needle from her straight needles. Robert attached the ends of the straight needles to a bit of tubing, and the afghan was finished in short order. Linstead wondered about the possibility of substituting different lengths of tubing to detachable tips to create an economical set of circulars in multiple sizes and lengths. In 1966, she patented a kit with a handy case that included different sized needle tips and different lengths of cable connectable by screw-in attachments. Thus, the NEEDLEMASTER— the precursor to the Denise Interchangeable Knitting Needles—was born.

≫→ KNITTING HISTORIAN AND AUTHOR **RICHARD RUTT** DONATED HIS EXTENSIVE COLLECTION OF KNITTING-RELATED MATERIALS—including vintage knitting booklets, patterns, articles, and magazines—to the University of Southampton Winchester School of Art Library. Rutt, the author of *A History of Hand Knitting*, wanted his collection joined with that of author Montse Stanley. Author JANE WALLER also donated her pattern collection, creating an incredible archive for hand knitters everywhere. A significant portion of the materials are available online for review.

Scottish folklore

names Nicnevin (known in some areas as Gyre-Carling) queen of the fairies, a kind of mother goddess/witch. It was said that if a woman left knitting or spinning unfinished at the New Year, Nicnevin would steal it. One source states that the Yule was one of Nicnevin's special days, and if a woman didn't finish her spinning before that day, Nicnevin would steal the fiber from her distaff to punish her for working on Nicnevin's holiday.

IN 2010, THE WORLD'S LARGEST SELBU MITTEN WAS KNITTED, a joint project of knitters from the organization Selbu Husflidslag, the Selbu Folk Museum, and the shop Selbu Husflid. A second mitten was finished in 2012, and the pair gained official Guinness World Records status. The mittens are knit in the same type of yarn used for regular-sized Selbu mittens using a 3mm/US 2 needle, and they are 6½ feet long.

In July 1545, the *Mary Rose*, King Henry VIII's flagship, sank north of the Isle of Wight.

Hundreds of men on board died as the damaged ship sank into the mucky ocean floor. There it sat, despite a few efforts to salvage it over the centuries, until 1982, when the Mary Rose Trust managed to raise it. Because conditions were just right, an extraordinary number of daily items were preserved and recovered from the wreck of the *Mary Rose*, including several knitted items or fragments. According to the Mary Rose Trust, three nearly complete woolen caps were found, each with a double brim and two lined in silk. Fragments of additional knitting were also found, indicating that knitters of this time period understood principles of shaping. A knitted tube approximately 1 foot long, knit in black wool in stockinette stitch, survived as well; it may have been some type of arm warmer or stocking/gaiter.

IN OUTER MONGOLIA, it's said that consuming a sheep eyeball pickled in tomato juice is a surefire cure for a hangover.

➤ Princess Diana was photographed wearing her famous Black Sheep sweater—a red pullover featuring white intarsia sheep with just one black sheep—in June 1981 at a polo match in Windsor. Designed by Sally Muir and Joanna Osborne, the sweater became inexorably associated with Princess Diana and her fashion legacy; the Victoria and Albert Museum added the original sweater, which was a gift to Diana from the mother of one of her page boys, to their collection in 1983. Knitters interested in making their own Black Sheep sweater can find the original pattern by Muir and Osborne available as a free download on Ravelry.com.

▼ ▼ ▼ ▼

A center-pull ball was once called a false clue.
(*Clew* is an old Anglo-Saxon word for a ball of yarn—perhaps the two terms are related.)

CELEBRITY KNITTERS
Classic Hollywood

Katharine Hepburn
•
Joan Crawford
•
Vivien Leigh
•
Ava Gardner
•
Doris Day
•
Ingrid Bergman
•
Sophia Loren
•
Debbie Reynolds
•
Lucille Ball
•
Audrey Hepburn
•
Ginger Rogers
•
Rita Hayworth
•
Carole Lombard
•
Marilyn Monroe
•
Edith Piaf

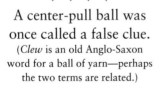

{ Author **Hans Christian Andersen** wrote a fairy tale called **"The Darning Needle"** about a, well, darning needle who fancied herself a bit above her station and came to a bad end. }

Grace Ennis

Grace Ennis was a California housewife who turned her passion for knitting socks, and later neckties, with novelty designs into a successful knitting pattern line. She started out by designing argyle socks for her husband, a Navy officer who loved her handknits. His friends on base loved them, too, so she began designing and knitting for others. Her designs eventually became so popular that she was dubbed "A Pretty Bel Air Blonde" whose work was full of "Socks Appeal" by the *Los Angeles Times*.

After Ennis's husband's friends and coworkers began ordering her creations, she decided to start her own business. Her company, Graphic Knitting Patterns, was established in 1946. With the money she earned from her first sales, Ennis hired a lithographer to print 500 copies of her patterns. The printer made a mistake—printing 2,000 instead—and there still weren't enough to fill all of Ennis's orders! Later, Ennis and her husband bought their own printing press and began printing the patterns from home. By 1955, Graphic Knitting Patterns was earning $200,000 a year in gross sales.

In November 1961, wildfires in Bel Air ravaged the Ennis home. Grace escaped without injury, but the home was destroyed. So were Ennis's patterns. Their homeowner's insurance wasn't enough to rebuild, so they moved to Santa Ana. Ennis tried reintroducing some of her patterns in 1963, but sales fizzled and she eventually closed the business.

Many years later, while preparing for another move, Ennis and a friend happily discovered that a box of patterns survived the fire. A retaining wall had fallen on the boxes, sheltering them from fire damage. Her friend vowed to begin selling the patterns again and was able to make them available for a time at a small number of knitting retailers.

Ennis's patterns feature traditional geometric designs like argyle, lattice, and diamond patterns, while others are also delightfully kitschy: a pipe with smoke rings, a surfer riding a wave, golf clubs, a cocktail, playing cards, a hot dog on a skewer, and many more. Her patterns can still be found at online auction sites. ✳

NOMENCLATURE FOR ANIMALS COMMONLY USED IN YARN CREATION

ALPACA	BUFFALO	CAMEL	GOAT
MALE sire or macho	**MALE** bull	**MALE** bull	**MALE** buck
FEMALE dam or hemra	**FEMALE** cow	**FEMALE** cow	**FEMALE** doe
BABY cria	**BABY** calf	**BABY** calf	**BABY** kid
GROUP herd	**GROUP** herd, gang, or obstinacy	**GROUP** caravan, flock, herd, or train	**GROUP** flock, herd, tribe, or trip
ADJECTIVE camelid	**ADJECTIVE** bubaline, bisontine	**ADJECTIVE** cameline	**ADJECTIVE** caprine, hircine

LLAMA	MUSK OX	RABBIT	SHEEP
MALE macho	**MALE** bull	**MALE** buck	**MALE** ram
FEMALE hemra	**FEMALE** cow	**FEMALE** doe	**FEMALE** ewe
BABY cria	**BABY** calf	**BABY** kit	**BABY** lamb
GROUP herd or flock	**GROUP** herd or cabinet	**GROUP** colony, warren, nest, down, husk, or herd	**GROUP** flock, drove, herd, drift, or down
ADJECTIVE camelid	**ADJECTIVE** bovine, ovibovine	**ADJECTIVE** leporine, lapine	**ADJECTIVE** ovine

YAK
MALE bull or boa
FEMALE dri or cow
BABY calf
GROUP herd
ADJECTIVE bosine

Shepherd's Bush is the name of a London Tube station, but the phrase's origins lie in the practice of pruning a hawthorn bush into a kind of topiary tree stand. By trimming the inner tree branches to form a platform, the outer branches form a protective ring. A shepherd could stand on the platform inside the bush and survey his flock while being sheltered from the elements.

⤳ Pioneers of the Printed Pattern

• Scottish designer JANE GAUGAIN (18?–1860), the daughter of a tailor, married a man who imported needlework items, and he began publishing her knitting patterns in 1837. Gaugain helped turn her husband's Edinburgh business into a thriving concern, and she is known for implementing a system of abbreviations that she used in her patterns. Unfortunately, her system of abbreviations did not catch on, and abbreviations fell out of use until the 20th century. Gaugain's best-known work is *The Lady's Assistant*, which was published in 22 editions; by the time of her death, she had published 16 books of knitting patterns, which did much to popularize knitting among the stylish ladies of Edinburgh.

• CORNELIA MEE (1815–1875), along with her husband and sister, ran a needlework business in Bath, England. Mee published her first book, *The Manual of Knitting, Netting, and Crochet*, in 1842, which contained various "receipts" or patterns for common household items. She continued to publish crochet and knitting patterns and was extremely influential in the English knitting and crochet world. At one point, she claimed to have invented crochet, and she included many patterns that were designed for charity knitting, which she called "making warm things for the poor." Her series *The Knitter's Companion* was published in 11 different editions over a 14-year period and sold approximately 55,000 copies.

• FRANCES LAMBERT'S background is shadowy, but we do know that she began publishing needlework manuals as early as 1842, when *The Hand-Book of Needlework* appeared. Lambert is considered one of the first writers to pay attention to gauge, although her advice was for knitters to work everything at "medium tension" rather than to specify a number of stitches per inch. Lambert also created one of the first knitting gauges, advised knitters to slip the first stitch of each row for a selvedge edge (she called it an "edge stitch"), and discussed the origin of the phrase *brioche knitting*.

• ELÉONORE RIEGO DE LA BRANCHARDIÈRE was also said to have been the creator of crochet, and indeed, she wrote more about crochet than knitting. It was said that she was of Irish descent and had a particular interest in developing Irish crochet lace. Her work *The Knitting Book*, published in 1847, contained illustrated instructions for how to knit—something her fellow authors tended not to include as it was assumed that a well-bred lady would already know the basics of knitting. She won many medals for her crochet work and wrote about knitting, lacework, and tatting as well as crochet. ✳

Most knitters are familiar with yarns made of cotton, wool, silk, and synthetic fibers like acrylic. Even yarns made of linen, angora, alpaca, cashmere, bamboo, and mohair are easy to find in today's global marketplace. But have you knit with yarn made with fiber from camels, llamas, yaks, bison, or musk ox? How about yarns derived from cellulose (often called rayon or tencel), sugar cane, milk, soy, or corn?

Or possibly plants other than cotton, like hemp, nettles, flax, or banana stalks?

Or the fiber of species not native to the United States, like the brushtail possum of New Zealand?

Yarn made with stainless steel?

Yarn containing seaweed fiber or chitin, a substance made from shrimp and crab shells?

Or how about sticking closer to home and spinning your own yarn made with the hair of your beloved dog or cat?

⟫→ The first issue of *Vogue Knitting*'s reboot (released for Fall/Winter 1982) featured 47 patterns knitted in 51 different yarns. Of the 51 yarns used in that issue, only one can be purchased today: Manos del Uruguay handspun wool, now called Manos del Uruguay Wool Clasica. In fact, as of press time, you could still purchase three of the original six colors called for in the pattern: Petrol, Steel, and Silica.

● ● ●

Two other yarns from that first issue are also available in similar form today. You can still purchase Lopi Léttlopi, an Icelandic wool yarn now sold by Westminster Fibers. Tahki Donegal Tweed is still with us in worsted-weight form, though the bulky-weight version shown in the magazine has been discontinued.

A Norwegian artist named Siren Elise Wilhelmsen created a clock that knits as it tells time.

The project, called "365 Knitting Clock," creates one stitch every half hour and, at the end of one year, has knit a 2-meter-long scarf. Once you learn the clock's unique system, you can use it to tell time even though it lacks the numbers and hands of a traditional clock.

■ ■ ■ ■

AMERICAN VS. BRITISH • EUROPEAN
KNITTING TERMS

AMERICAN	BRITISH • EUROPEAN
gauge	tension
bind off	cast off
stockinette stitch	stocking stitch
seed stitch	moss stitch
yarn over	may distinguish between yarn over, yarn round needle/yarn over needle, yarn forward
work even	work straight

AMERICAN VS. BRITISH • EUROPEAN
CROCHET TERMS

AMERICAN	BRITISH • EUROPEAN
single crochet	double crochet
half double crochet	half treble crochet
double crochet	treble crochet
treble crochet	double treble crochet
double treble crochet	triple treble crochet
triple treble crochet	quadruple treble crochet
fasten off	cast off
skip	miss
yarn over	yarn over hook

The first recorded wool shop—that is, a shop devoted to selling knitting wool as opposed to selling wool in addition to other clothing and/or housewares—was founded in Glasgow, Scotland, in 1796.

■ ■ ■ ■

UNUSUAL NAMES FOR
VINTAGE YARN

If you think today's yarn colors have unusual names, rest assured that there is nothing new under the sun. During Victorian times, fashion houses and clothing manufacturers had a penchant for using phrases like "elephant's breath" to describe specific hues, leading the *New York Times*, in a 1908 article, to discuss the "quaint, grotesque, and absurd terms used to describe the most delicate tints." Elizabethan color names were often just as, well, colorful. Who wouldn't want a gown that was the color of a "Dead Spaniard"? Other color names from bygone eras:

- **Paris en feu** ("Paris on fire") = a red shade with orange and brown

- **Flea (also called "puce")** = a brown or purplish-brown color

- **Carbuncle** = deep red

- **Puke** = a brownish-green

- **Milk-and-water** = bluish-white

- **Popinjay** = bright green or blue

- **Watchet** = pale blue-green

- **Laylock** = warm pink

- **Murrey** = purplish-red

- **Goose turd** = yellowish green

- **Mousse d'eau** = described by *Woman's World* magazine as "closely resembling the scum which rises on a marshy pool"

- **Abraham** = dark or dingy yellow

- **Ashes of roses** = grayish mauve

- **Stifled sigh** = mauve and pale blue

- **Gluten** = deep cream

- **Pigeon neck** = mauve or lilac

- **Lustie-gallant** = light red

- **Fly's Wing** = dark gray

(In case you were wondering, "elephant's breath"
was variously described as olive, blue, and grayish, while
"Dead Spaniard" was a light grayish-tan.)

➤ In the book *Yorkshire Wit, Character, Folklore and Customs*, published in 1898, author Richard Blakeborough describes an old Yorkshire, England, custom involving knitted garters:

If the youngest daughter in a family is married first,
the eldest had better unravel one of her garters; knitting
the same, mixed with other wool, into something a
man can wear. This she must present to the one she has special
regard for, and it will most likely incline his heart to her.

THE KNITTERS OF THE ANDES MOUNTAINS
(MODERN-DAY PERU AND BOLIVIA) ARE RENOWNED
FOR CREATING WARM AND COLORFUL CAPS CALLED
CHULLOS.

Called *ch'ullus* in the regional Quechua language and *llucho* in
the regional Aymara language, chullos are thick knitted caps with
earflaps, and they appear in a staggering variety of colors and designs.
Pompoms or tassels are often attached to the top of the cap or to the
ties. Traditionally in the Andes, hats with earflaps are worn nearly
exclusively by men and boys, while girls wear caps with ruffles.
Interestingly, despite the notoriety of chullos, it's believed that knitting
was not practiced in this region until the 16th century,
when Spanish and Portuguese explorers introduced the craft to the
indigenous people of South America.

VIRGIN WOOL has nothing to do with a sheep's dating
history, but simply refers to wool that has never been used before.
It's fresh off the sheep and is also called new wool.
Because wool is such a durable fiber, it can be reused either by
collecting old wool garments or using remnants and waste from
processing. This is called recycled wool or shoddy, and it creates
a product with shorter fibers than those of the original wool.
For this reason, recycled wool is often mixed with a longer staple
fiber to increase overall fiber length.

A steek is a method used by knitters to knit a sweater body entirely in the round, as a tube.

✂ The sweater is then cut open at the armholes
to add sleeves, and/or at the center front to form
the two front pieces of a cardigan. The word is
derived from the Scottish *steek*, meaning
to fasten or close. How can one cut through
knitting without the stitches unraveling?
By making a smart yarn choice (best choices are
wools with a tendency to mesh together, such as
those made from Shetland or Icelandic breeds)
and by using reinforcing techniques like hand- or
machine-sewing along either side of the cut, or
using knotting or crochet instead of sewing to
ensure that the stitches stay firmly in place.

☛ Not all worsted-spun yarns are knit at worsted weight, and not all worsted-weight yarns are worsted-spun. Confused? The term *worsted* is used to refer to two completely different concepts when it comes to yarn.

One type of *worsted* refers to the process of how wool yarn is spun. Wool yarn can be spun using a process called woolen spinning, or it can be spun using a process called worsted spinning. Woolen spinning involves carding but not combing fibers—that means that the individual fibers are not perfectly parallel but are jumbled around in different directions. Woolen yarns tend to be less even in thickness and are often made with wool that has relatively short individual fibers. The yarn is soft and can often be pulled apart without much trouble. In worsted spinning, the process takes longer, as the fiber is not only carded but also combed to remove fibers that are shorter and rougher and to make the fibers lie parallel to each other. The end product is a smoother, stronger yarn, with a very even thickness.

The worsted-versus-woolen distinction has to do with spinning yarn. The other use of the term *worsted* has to do with a yarn's weight and the approximate gauge at which it knits. The Craft Yarn Council, an industry group, has created a standard yarn weight system. The term *worsted* is often used to refer to Category 4 of the CYC's system, meaning yarns that knit at around 16 to 20 sts over 4 inches/10cm on size US 7–9 needles. It is the most common weight of yarn used by knitters. Thus, *worsted* in this context has nothing to do with how the yarn is made but rather is a way to identify its thickness and approximate gauge. ✳

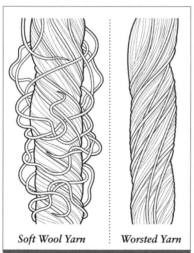

Soft Wool Yarn   *Worsted Yarn*

THE TOP 10 KNITTING PROJECTS

As measured by appearing the most times as an ongoing project in users' Ravelry queues:

1. **Baby Surprise Jacket** by Elizabeth Zimmermann (baby jacket)

2. **Clapotis** by Kate Gilbert (scarf/stole)

3. **Fetching** by Cheryl Niamath (fingerless gloves)

4. **Hitchhiker** by Martina Behm (scarf)

5. **Honey Cowl** by Antonia Shankland (cowl)

6. **Monkey** by Cookie A. (socks)

7. **Calorimetry** by Kathryn Schoendorf (headscarf)

8. **Turn a Square** by Jared Flood (hat)

9. **GAPtastic Cowl** by Jen Geigley

10. **Saartje's Booties** by Saartje DeBruijn (baby booties)

According to knitting expert MARY THOMAS, the first knitting needles were made of copper wire with a hook at one end, and were used in Arabian and Mediterranean countries. We know that the hookless needles we're familiar with today were in use by the 12th or 13th centuries based on artifacts and paintings. Early knitting needles were made out of whatever substances the knitter could find: bone, ivory, wood, wire, bamboo, and steel. Modern needles may use untraditional substances like carbon, glass, acrylic, casein (a protein derived from milk), aluminum, and plastic. ∾

You've heard of pita bread, but have you heard of pita lace? In the Azores Islands, fiber from the *Agave americana* plant (also called the century plant) was used to make yarn called pita. Over time, the phrase *pita lace* became associated with extremely fine knitted lace patterns from the Azores, regardless of what type of yarn was used.

Fiber-Related
Bumper Stickers

IT'S NOT A HOBBY; IT'S A POST-APOCALYPTIC LIFE SKILL.

I knit so I do not kill people.

GOT WOOL?

CAUTION: HOOKER ON BOARD.

Life is too short for knitting with cheap yarn.

Friends don't let friends knit drunk.

KNIT FAST, DIE WARM.

Knit happens.

KEEP CALM AND CARRY YARN.

She who dies with the most yarn wins.

SPINNING: BECAUSE KNITTING ISN'T WEIRD ENOUGH.

Yarn: cheaper than crack. Usually.

KNITTING TAKES BALLS.

Veni Vidi Acubus Texui. (I came, I saw, I knitted.)

Eat. Knit. Love.

Spinners do it with a twist.

MY OTHER CAR IS A LOOM.

SO MUCH YARN, SO LITTLE TIME.

☞ **Basque sheepherders** who immigrated to the western United States created a series of tree carvings called arborglyphs. Sheepherders spent the summer months camping out with sheep in isolated country, devoid of most human contact for lengthy periods of time. They began leaving carvings on aspen trees to signal good watering ground, record events, or to simply record their initials, names, and/or original hometowns. Some sheepherders created images of animals, people, or objects and recorded their movements, creating a fascinating record for historians who can use the carvings to track the movement of the herders and their flocks.

THE NBC TELEVISION COMEDY *30 ROCK* INCLUDES AN EPISODE WHERE CHARACTER JENNA SINGS AT A MYTHICAL COLLEGE FOOTBALL GAME CALLED THE WOOL BOWL.

Behind her, a strange mascot named Woollie bops and sways. Woollie appears again in a scene (along with an animatronic sheep) where Jenna meets with the president of the Wool Council to discuss becoming a brand ambassador. During the episode, the president of the Wool Council, played by Victor Garber, announces that things are *"very wool."*

Old folk rhymes for counting sheep have existed in various districts of England for centuries. The "numbers" that make up each rhyme are similar, with minor regional differences.

In Wensleydale, for example, sheep were counted, from one to nine, using the following: **yan, tean, tither, mither, pip, teaser, leaser, catra, horna.** The count usually ended with 20, then a mark would be made on a stick or on the ground so that the shepherd could count his sheep by 20s, or scores.

As of spring 2014, the handknitting yarn currently in production in the most colors was JAMIESON'S SHETLAND SPINDRIFT 2-PLY, a fingering weight (CYC Category 1) yarn, made entirely of Shetland wool grown and spun in the Shetland Islands.

WILLIAM LEE:
💙 *Spurned for a Skein*

If your significant other complains that you're more interested in your knitting than in him or her, tell the story of the Reverend William Lee. Lee was a 16th-century English curate who invented the stocking frame, a machine for knitting stockings, supposedly because the girl he was courting was more interested in her knitting than in him.

> *THE CURATE IS SAID TO HAVE FALLEN DEEPLY IN LOVE WITH A YOUNG LADY OF THE VILLAGE, who failed to reciprocate his affections; and when he visited her, she was accustomed to pay much more attention to the process of* **knitting stockings and instructing her pupils in the art, than to the addresses of her admirer.** *This slight is said to have created in his mind such an aversion to knitting by hand, that he formed the determination to invent a machine that should supersede it and render it a gainless employment. For three years he devoted himself to the prosecution of the invention, sacrificing everything to his new idea. At the prospect of success opened before him, he abandoned his curacy, and devoted himself to the art of stocking making by machinery.*
>
> – SAMUEL SMILES, *SELF-HELP* (1859)

WE DON'T KNOW IF THIS STORY IS TRUE, and it has also been suggested that Reverend Lee was motivated more by economic duress than because he believed his lady friend was neglecting him. This version of the Lee legend says that Lee violated a rule of his college that prohibited curates from marrying. He therefore lost his job. According to this version of events, his wife—who was a fast and skilled knitter—began earning money from her knitting to support the couple. Lee spent a great deal of time watching her needles moving, which led him to experiment with creating a mechanized method of knitting.

Regardless of Lee's motivation, he did in fact create a knitting machine, made largely of wood, that mimicked the motion of the human hands as they knit. His invention is generally regarded as a major advance in the early days of the Industrial Revolution. Once his machine was up and running, Lee began producing machine-knit stockings, and several of his relatives (including a brother, James) joined him in the business.

REVEREND LEE WENT ON TO SEEK A PATENT for his stocking-knitting machine, hoping to enjoy an official monopoly on the process of machine-knitting stockings. (At the time, British monarchs issued patents to inventors often as a method of awarding a monopoly to favored petitioners.) Lee demonstrated his machine to the queen, but she refused to award him a patent, her well-known love of silk stockings notwithstanding, on the ground that it would cause hand knitters to be unemployed. Thus Reverend Lee ended up a victim of an early case of trade protectionism.

LEE'S STRUGGLE TO POPULARIZE AND PROFIT from his invention took another strange turn when King Henry IV of France entered the picture. The wily French monarch invited Lee to bring his machine to Rouen, a center of French manufacturing. Lee settled in France in 1605, taking machines and workers with him. He faced another serious setback when his benefactor, King Henry IV, was stabbed to death; without Henry's support, Lee could not obtain the protection from the French court that he had been promised, and he died in France poor and discouraged. ✳

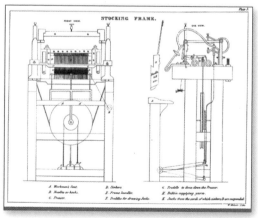

Technical drawing of William Lee's knitting frame

Rest in peace, Shrek.

The world said good-bye to the New Zealand sheep named Shrek in June 2011 when Shrek succumbed to age-related illnesses. Shrek became famous in 2004 when he was captured after hiding for six years in caves on the South Island of New Zealand. By that time, the Merino sheep's fleece was gigantic, weighing about 60 pounds. (The typical fleece of a sheep like Shrek weighs less than 10 pounds.) Shrek's fleece was said to contain enough wool for 20 men's suits! His owner, John Perriam, told a local television station that Shrek "was just an ordinary sheep, went AWOL and hid, and when he was found he became the darling of the nation." Shrek was shorn on television and his huge fleece was auctioned off, with the proceeds going to children's medical charities.

WHAT CAN BE MADE FROM A BALE OF COTTON?

- **215** pairs of blue jeans
- **690** bath towels
- **2,104** pairs of boxer shorts
- **1,256** pillowcases
- **3,085** diapers
- **21,960** handkerchiefs
- **313,600** $100 bills

As this book went to press, the yarn listed in the most projects on Ravelry.com was RED HEART SUPER SAVER, a worsted-weight acrylic yarn used in a whopping 178,223 different projects. Ravelry members have made everything from afghans to stuffed toys, baby dresses to holiday stockings, and even festive flowers to adorn a bird feeder out of this yarn. What natural-fiber yarn is used in the most projects? CASCADE 220, a worsted-weight all-wool yarn, appears in 132,618 projects. Cotton lovers were working on 98,647 projects in the top cotton choice, LILY SUGAR 'N CREAM, another worsted-weight yarn.

Richard the Lionheart was captured by his enemies when he returned from the Crusades. It's often said that Richard's ransom was paid in wool. King Henry VI, Richard's captor, demanded a huge ransom—the equivalent of three years of income—for the British monarchy. A great effort went out to find the resources to pay for Richard's return. One source: Cistercian monasteries that were asked to donate wool. Thus it is said that Richard's ransom was paid with 50,000 sacks of English wool.

☛ TABLE SHOWING NUMBER OF LOOMS
AND YARDS OF LINEN MANUFACTURED IN EIGHT
TOWNSHIPS OF PENNSYLVANIA IN 1810

	Looms	Yards of linen cloth	Yards of woolen cloth	Yards of cotton cloth
Kingston	25	6,135	1,827	93
Plymouth	42	7,847	1,762	91
Pittston	28	5,740	1,690	59
Wilkes-Barre	33	6,531	1,717	129
Exeter	31	3,771	1,394	80
Abington	39	2,485	1,429	34
Providence	36	5,643	1,430	147
Hanover	25	5,369	1,291	69

United States Marine Squadron 214 is better known as the
BLACK SHEEP SQUADRON.

 The group of flyers was organized during World War II under Major Gregory "Pappy" Boyington in the South Pacific in 1943. Originally consisting of pilots not associated with other squadrons, the members flew borrowed planes until they were given permission to form an official squadron with the caveat that they had to be ready for combat in just four weeks. Ready they were. The squadron fought valiantly, earning the Presidential Unit Citation for extraordinary heroism in action. Although the original members disbanded after their second tour of action, the squadron has continued to exist, fighting to the current day. Their insignia features an image of a black horned ram. The exploits of Major Boyington's original squadron were dramatized in the American television show *Baa Baa Black Sheep*.

US President Gerald R. Ford was *given a sweater handknit in red, white, and blue yarn, featuring a colorwork motif of "WIN"* in support of Ford's "Whip Inflation Now" campaign. The name of the donor and the date received are not known.

SHETLAND TERMS USED IN SPINNING

- **rock:** vernacular term for a spindle

- **muckle wheel:** a large spinning wheel, relatively simple in structure, used for centuries in Shetland; it had no distaff or treadle

- **Norrawa wheel:** more complex spinning wheel, often imported to Shetland from Norway, with a treadle and distaff

- **Shetland spinney:** a castle-style wheel especially useful for spinning finer weights of yarn

- **teasing:** process of picking wool with the fingers before carding and spinning

- **twining:** plying

- **cairds:** carders, used to prepare wool for spinning woolen-style

- **kems:** combs, used to prepare wool for spinning worsted-style

- **hesptree (or reel):** niddy-noddy

◻ ◻ ◻ It's a question that has been asked numerous times since the post-9/11 tightening of airline security: can a knitter take knitting needles onto an airplane?

A January 2013 statement from the TSA unequivocally states:

> *"Knitting needles are permitted in your carry-on baggage or checked baggage."* (Emphasis theirs.)

The TSA website even includes a handy stock photo of some metal knitting needles and yarn. Note that circular thread cutters or any other devices with internal blades are not allowed in carry-ons and must be placed in checked bags. While this is welcome news for those leaving from an American airport (assuming the individual TSA agent is aware of the current rule), if you're leaving from an international airport, you may not be so lucky. Different countries have different rules about whether knitting needles are allowed in carry-on bags; for example, while the Heathrow Airport website states that knitting needles are allowed in carry-on items, French rules prohibit the carrying of knitting needles and require them to be stored in checked luggage. Too bad the writers of the television show *NCIS* didn't do their research: in the episode "Jet Lag," which aired in 2010, a plane leaving Paris is the setting for a murder committed with—yep, a knitting needle.

▼ ▼ ▼ ▼

When we think of Icelandic knits, the **lopi** sweater, or **lopapeysa,** immediately comes to mind.

Knit in the round with a yoke and featuring borders around wrists and hemline, the lopapeysa is a symbol of Iceland to both tourists and Icelanders alike. The sweaters are traditionally knit from the wool of Icelandic sheep, a long-haired breed with wool that is warm, strong, and water-repellent. You might think that a sweater so beloved and so closely associated with a country has been around for centuries, but the lopapeysa is a relatively recent creation believed to have been created in the 1950s by an unknown designer or group of designers. The first lopapeysa were knit with vibrant colors, but the style has evolved to feature muted tones of gray, brown, black, and ivory that reflect the natural colors of Icelandic sheep.

We've all heard of sheepdogs guarding their flock, but some farmers and agricultural groups are looking to llamas—yes, llamas—to protect the herd.

Llamas have an instinctive dislike for canines, which means they react strongly and aggressively to the presence of canine predators like coyotes. Llama guards will sound an alarm when coyotes appear, then attempt to chase the coyote or other predator away, even kicking it to make it retreat. While use of llamas to guard flocks is not widespread, it remains another tool in the hands of farmers seeking to prevent loss of their animals to nearby predators.

WHIMSICAL HEADGEAR

ELIZABETH ZIMMERMANN ONCE WROTE,

"And this brings me to hats. To which the sky is the limit.
People will put anything on their heads, it seems to me for two reasons:
either it keeps them warm or it makes them feel cute."

A survey of hat patterns on the website Ravelry.com
reveals headgear shaped like:

owls

berries, apples,
pineapples, pumpkins

fish

porcupine
(with quills, natch)

chicken heads

dinosaurs

bears, bunnies, kittens,
and puppies

cowboy hat, top hat,
jester hat, Santa hat,
pirate hat, elf hat,
and nurse hat

wizard and witch hats

Christmas trees

the Grinch

monsters

candy corn

Thanksgiving turkeys

cupcakes

cornrows

slugs

faux beards

princess hat with
crown and braids

sharks

leprechauns

sock monkeys

baseballs

spiderwebs

a human brain

Medusa's hair

a unicorn with a
rainbow mane

a Viking hat,
and a chicken
Viking hat

Chicken Viking Hat
pattern by Sarah Mundy

■ ■ ■ ■ THE 1969 FILM *MIDNIGHT COWBOY*, WHICH
WON THREE ACADEMY AWARDS AND IS STILL THE ONLY
X-RATED MOVIE TO HAVE WON A BEST PICTURE OSCAR,
OWES ITS MAKING TO DESIGNER **KAFFE FASSETT**.
Fassett had met director John Schlesinger in London and was impressed
with his directorial ability. When a friend gave Fassett the book
Midnight Cowboy to read, he thought it begged to be made into a film
and gave the book to Schlesinger. After the film's success,
Schlesinger gave Fassett a "finder's fee" of 5,000 pounds for
bringing the book to his attention.

> The Karoo region of South Africa produces more mohair than any other part of the world. And all because of a sultan's mistake.

In 1838, Sultan Mahmoud II of Turkey sent Angora goats—12 rams and one ewe—to Port Elizabeth, South Africa. The rams were neutered, and the sultan believed the ewe to be infertile. Unfortunately for the sultan, who wanted to maintain a monopoly on the export of mohair fiber, the ewe happened to be pregnant, and she gave birth to a kid on the trip to South Africa. Thus the mohair industry in South Africa was born.

IN 1739, ELIZA LUCAS PINCKNEY was placed in charge of her family's three South Carolina plantations at the tender age of 16. Her father, who was in the Caribbean at the time, frequently sent her different types of seeds to see how they would grow, with the hope of discovering a plant that would make a good cash crop. In 1739, he sent her indigo seeds. Although Eliza was not immediately successful growing the indigo, eventually she had a successful growing year, and she began experimenting with extracting the dye from the indigo. As a result of her efforts, indigo became a major cash crop, revolutionizing the economy of the colony. George Washington was one of the pallbearers at her funeral, and she was the first woman to be inducted into the South Carolina Business Hall of Fame.

◆ ◆ ◆ ◆ ◆

KNITTING UNIVERSITY

Need a few college credits? Consider the following courses:

Sheep & Goat Production and Management
(Penn State)

•

Anthropology of Handmade Commodities
(Yale)

•

Experimental Machine Knitting Workshop
(Morley College, London)

•

Patternmaking for Knit Garments
(FIT, New York)

•

Ecuador Boot Camp in Alpaca Husbandry
(University of Vermont)

•

Knitting and Philosophy
(University of South Carolina Honors College)

•

Knitting for Noobs
(Experimental College–Oberlin College)

➤ ICONIC SWEATERS IN
POP CULTURE

MR. ROGERS' CARDIGANS:
Fred Rogers, host of *Mr. Rogers' Neighborhood*, started each episode by changing into his sneakers and putting on a cardigan. Children found the routine comforting, and the cardigan sweater became indelibly associated with Mr. Rogers. Fred Rogers once said in an interview that his mother knitted all of his cardigans.

TACKY HOLIDAY SWEATERS:
Whether it's your grandmom, your favorite elementary school teacher, or your I-meant-it-ironically hipster friend, ornate holiday sweaters have become a thing. Even Colin Firth had trouble carrying off his garish reindeer sweater in *Bridget Jones's Diary*.

HARRY POTTER'S SWEATER:
Knitted by his friend Ron's mom in nubby tweed, Harry's first Weasley sweater was a touching gift that meant he was one of the family.

THE DUDE'S SWEATER FROM *THE BIG LEBOWSKI*:
It abides.

CHARLIE BROWN'S SWEATER:
It has inspired many homages (one as recently as 2013 by Michael Bastian). While its simple zigzag is forever associated with Charlie Brown, he doesn't wear the sweater in the very first comic strips where he was featured. Charlie began donning the sweater a few months after the first strips ran.

SCOOBY DOO'S VELMA:
She always wears her orange, tunic-length turtleneck.

PENGUIN SWEATERS:
About once a year, the Internet is filled with posts begging knitters and crocheters to make sweaters for penguins affected by ocean oil spills. Most appeals cite the need to keep smaller penguins from ingesting oil when they groom themselves until they are strong enough to be cleaned. In 2001, a Tasmanian wildlife conservation group ran a drive to collect sweaters for penguins and was quickly overwhelmed by the number received. Since then, other groups have made appeals for penguin sweaters, but a number of wildlife experts have stated that sweaters

aren't particularly useful for oil-soaked penguins. Most sweaters knit for penguins will end up dressing toy penguins, with the money raised from the sale of the toys used to benefit wildlife charities.

BERT AND ERNIE FROM SESAME STREET:
Are they sweaters or knit tops? Either way, the Muppet pals are usually clad in their iconic stripes.

STARSKY'S BELTED CARDIGAN:
Before there was *The Big Lebowski*, there was *Starsky & Hutch*, an American cop television show broadcast from 1975 to 1979. The bulky belted cardigan known as "the Starsky" was originally worn by actor Paul Michael Glaser on the show, and it was reportedly based on a Mexican sweater pattern.

THE KID FROM THE SHINING:
His light blue sweater featured an intarsia rocket ship with "Apollo 11" embroidered on it. After filming was complete, the sweater was purchased by a crew member; she wanted it for her nephew. Oddly, the reference to Apollo 11 was interpreted by some conspiracy theorists as an admission by director Stanley Kubrick that he helped fake moon landing videos. (Kubrick's assistant called the theory "balderdash," noting that a friend of the costume designer knitted it since Kubrick wanted Danny to wear something handmade.) ✳

▼ ▼ ▼ ▼
The Old English Sheepdog,
sometimes called the shepherd's dog or the bobtailed sheepdog, is a breed recognized by the American Kennel Club.

It is believed the breed was developed in the early 1800s in England, probably bred from the Scottish Bearded Collie and the Russian Owtchar. The breed is large, with a shaggy gray or white coat, long flat ears, and a furry face. Famous fictional Old English Sheepdogs include Barkley (*Sesame Street*); Elwood (*The Shaggy D.A.*); Tiger (*The Patty Duke Show*); Max (*The Little Mermaid*); and Edison (*Chitty Chitty Bang Bang*).

IS IT A SWEATER
OR A JUMPER?

The Oxford English Dictionary dates the first use
of the term *sweater* to 1828, referring to garments covering a
horse during training to make the horse sweat.

● ● ●

By the end of the 19th century, *sweater* was widely used to refer to a
vest or jersey, usually woolen, either worn by athletes during exercise to
increase sweating and thereby reduce their weight, or put on before or
after exercising to prevent the athlete from becoming chilled.

● ● ●

The term *jumper* was commonly used in England in the 1800s to
refer to a loose-fitting shirt or jacket that reached the hips.
The OED states that *jumper* was derived from the term *jump* or
jumps, used for a man's short coat or a woman's tunic.
(*Jump* itself may be derived from the French word *juppe*,
meaning women's jacket or bodice.)

The first mammal to be cloned from an adult body cell was a sheep named Dolly.

Born in 1996, Dolly was once called "the world's most famous sheep."
She spent her entire life in Edinburgh, Scotland, but died before
her seventh birthday. Dolly was a Finn-Dorset sheep and was named
after country singer Dolly Parton; scientist Ian Wilmut was quoted as
saying, "Dolly is derived from a mammary gland cell and we couldn't
think of a more impressive pair of glands than Dolly Parton's."

Amounts of Wool Produced Globally Each Year

United States
less than
26,700
metric tons

China
400,000
metric tons

New
Zealand
165,000
metric tons

Australia
362,100
metric tons

United
Kingdom
68,000
metric tons

∽ LACE KNITTING TERMS

BOBBLE:
a group of stitches worked together to form a small ball that protrudes from the surface of the knitting

DRESSING:
also called blocking, the method of washing and stretching a fabric to smooth out imperfections, obtain the correct dimensions, and emphasize the stitch pattern

EYELET:
a small hole intentionally placed in a knitted fabric, often by use of a yarnover

FAGOTTING OR FAGGOTTING:
an open, mesh-like stitch in which every stitch is either a yarnover or a decrease

INSERT:
a motif that is placed or inserted between sections of a knitted piece; often a vertical motif

LIFELINE:
a thin thread that is knit along with the working yarn as a precaution in case the knitter needs to unravel stitches. The lifeline makes it easier to replace the stitches in an intricate pattern in their correct order and placement. May be made of crochet thread, embroidery floss, sewing thread, fishing line, or even dental floss.

MEDALLION:
a knitted fabric worked in the round and blocked flat to form a circular or polygonal shape

PICOT:
a tiny point or rounded peak at the edge of a garment, often worked through a special cast-on or bind-off method

---

▶First Lady Grace Coolidge,

an avid and talented knitter, won honorable mention in a national needlecrafting contest sponsored by the Fleisher Yarn Company in 1923. Her "Slumberland Afghan" was knit in pink and white Germantown yarn and lined with pink crepe de chine. Because the entrants' names did not appear on their submissions, the judges—who included the editors of top needlework magazines—did not know who had knit the baby blanket.

YARN COLOR EFFECTS

Marled yarn

is made of two or more plies of different colors twisted together.
If the individual plies are close in value and hue, the effect will be
muted; if not, the effect can be bright and eye-catching. Sometimes
marled yarns contain one or more white plies twisted with
colored plies to give a barber pole effect.

◆ ◆ ◆

Ragg yarns

are a type of marled yarn originating in Scandinavia;
generally ragg yarns are sturdy yarns made by combining
white plies with brown plies. The term *ragg* is probably
derived from the Norwegian *raggsokk*, meaning a heavy
sock made of coarse, sturdy wool.

◆ ◆ ◆

Heathered yarns

are predominantly one color with flecks or small areas of a different
color, or a different shade of the main color, showing throughout.
The heathered effect is created by mixing two different colors or shades
of fiber together. For example, a mill may combine white wool with
beige wool, or gray wool with light brown wool, and then dye the result.
The different constituent colors in the yarn will appear as different
shades of the dye color used.

◆ ◆ ◆

Self-patterning yarns

are specially dyed so that when they are knitted up at a
standard gauge, they form patterns. The knitter need not
change yarn, follow a chart or pattern, or strand multiple
skeins of yarn to create fairly intricate patterns like Fair
Isle motifs, checkerboards, or jacquards.

◆ ◆ ◆

Ombré yarns

feature multiple shades of the same hue gradating from light to dark. The colors may change from one shade to the next slowly, forming wide stripes of color, or quickly, giving a less regular effect.

❖ ❖ ❖

Tweed

Sometimes a mill or handspinner will add small bits of fiber, in complementary or contrasting colors, to a yarn during the spinning process. This creates little bumps or flecks of color called *neps* and the resulting yarn is called *tweed*.

❖ ❖ ❖

Self-striping yarns

are typically dyed in long stretches of color; when knit up, each length of color produces multiple rows or rounds of knitting, creating stripes. Stripes may be wide or thin, depending on how long each individual stretch of color runs. Some self-striping yarns are made by plying: fiber is dyed in different colors, then the mill spins a segment using one color of the fiber, then gradually transitions to the second color, and so on. Or the mill may begin by using multiple plies of the same color, then switch to the next color, one ply at a time, to create gradually morphing stripes.

❖ ❖ ❖

Variegated

means multicolored and refers to yarns that contain multiple colors of dye, usually in relatively small lengths across the strand. Variegated yarns allow the knitter to change the color of stitches quickly, without using multiple skeins of solid-colored yarns and without having to strand colors or weave in multiple ends. Sometimes variegated yarns are called space-dyed yarns.

❖ ❖ ❖

MATCH THE SLOGAN
TO THE FIBER-RELATED ENTITY THAT COINED IT

• SLOGAN	• ENTITY
1. America's Yarn Shop	Lorna's Laces
2. The fabric of our lives	Alchemy
3. Little purls of wisdom	Cotton Incorporated
4. Yarn + life + fun	Louet
5. We make pretty string.	Imperial Stock Ranch
6. The American wool tradition	Fiber Factor
7. Where my stitches at?	WEBS
8. The ultimate knitting event	Craftsy.com
9. Yarns of transformation	Knitting Daily
10. Learn it. Make it.	Schoppel
11. Passion for yarn	Ravelry.com
12. Where life meets knitting	Knitty.com
13. Will you swatch or will you watch?	*Knit Simple* magazine
14. Make it your own	Vogue Knitting LIVE

CORRECT ANSWERS

1. WEBS; **2.** Cotton Inc.; **23** Knitty.com; **4.** *Knit Simple* magazine;
5. Lorna's Laces; **6.** Imperial Stock Ranch; **7.** Ravelry.com; **8.** Vogue
Knitting LIVE; **0.** Alchemy; **10.** Craftsy.com; **11.** Schoppel;
12. Knitting Daily; **13.** Fiber Factor; **13.** Louet

SUPERMODELS AND CELEBRITIES WHO HAVE
WORN GARMENTS IN THE PAGES OF *VOGUE KNITTING*
• Cindy Crawford *(Spring/Summer 1986; Holiday 1986)*
• Paulina Porizkova *(Spring/Summer 1984; Holiday 2007 cover)*
• Stephanie Seymour *(Holiday 1986)*
• Jennifer Flavin *(Crochet 1994)*
• Daryl Hannah *(Fall 2003 cover)*
• Courtney Thorne-Smith *(Spring/Summer 2005)*
• McKey Sullivan *(America's Next Top Model cycle 11 winner, Fall 2009)*
• Martha Stewart *(Holiday 2011 cover)*

NEW ZEALAND'S

first locally published knitting pattern book was called *Her Excellency's Knitting Book,* and it appeared in August 1915. The author was Annette Foljambe (known as Lady Liverpool), and the book was intended to motivate New Zealand women to continue knitting socks, balaclavas, and other warm items for soldiers serving in World War I.

THE PHRASE "STICK TO YOUR KNITTING" is used in the business world to refer to a conservative approach, or continuing to do what has always been done well rather than venturing into areas beyond one's expertise. The expression has been used at least since the late 1800s; a pharmaceutical journal dated 1898 admonished those in advertising to keep references to the ongoing war out of advertising:

"There is a homely old injunction which originated in our homespun days which the advertiser might recall. It is this: Stick to your knitting."

EISAKU NORO, owner and founder of the NORO YARN company, has said that he can discern qualities of wool such as staple length, thickness, and suppleness by touch alone, with his eyes shut.

Names for Knitting Mistakes

DOWN LOOP
accidentally knitting through the loops of two rows at one time

•

BACK BAR
skipping a stitch so that an unknitted loop appears on the wrong side of the work

•

LADDER
the effect of a dropped stitch that has unraveled back several rows

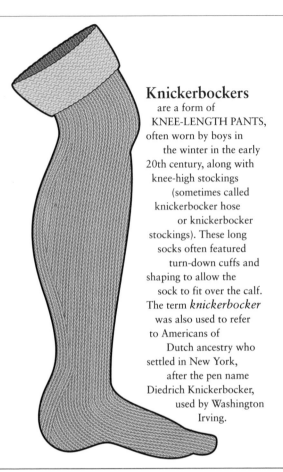

Knickerbockers

are a form of KNEE-LENGTH PANTS, often worn by boys in the winter in the early 20th century, along with knee-high stockings (sometimes called knickerbocker hose or knickerbocker stockings). These long socks often featured turn-down cuffs and shaping to allow the sock to fit over the calf. The term *knickerbocker* was also used to refer to Americans of Dutch ancestry who settled in New York, after the pen name Diedrich Knickerbocker, used by Washington Irving.

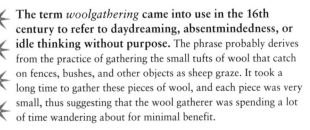

The term *woolgathering* came into use in the 16th century to refer to daydreaming, absentmindedness, or idle thinking without purpose. The phrase probably derives from the practice of gathering the small tufts of wool that catch on fences, bushes, and other objects as sheep graze. It took a long time to gather these pieces of wool, and each piece was very small, thus suggesting that the wool gatherer was spending a lot of time wandering about for minimal benefit.

I N THE EARLY 1980s, bumper stickers reading "Let knitters do it at home" began appearing on cars in Vermont. The bumper stickers weren't just a coy way for knitters to represent, but instead protested a decades-old US Department of Labor regulation that prohibited "home work."

AN OBSCURE PROVISION of the 1938 Fair Labor Standards Act—a key piece of federal legislation that established a uniform minimum wage, maximum 40-hour work week, and other employee protections—banned workers from doing several types of work at home, including knitting and embroidery. The law was intended to prevent companies from circumventing minimum wage requirements by claiming that knitters and other crafters weren't employees and therefore fell outside federal regulation. But in 1979, when the Department of Labor began targeting women who knit ski caps for a Vermont manufacturer, it triggered outrage among those participating in the cottage industry. Knitters were highly skilled at creating caps and other items quickly, often on home machines, and wanted the flexibility they had in knitting at home, sandwiching their knitting work around other responsibilities such as child care. As a result of the protests, the Department of Labor rescinded its ban in 1981, only to have a federal appellate court reinstate it. In 1984, the ban on home knitting, as well as certain other specified types of home work, was lifted, although the Department of Labor maintained some regulation to ensure that employers could not outsource work to home workers in order to create mini-sweatshops.

TERMS USED TO DESCRIBE THE WOOL COLOR OF THE NAVAJO-CHURRO SHEEP BREED

- white shell: *mainly white, but with some tan or cream fibers*
- sand: *light beige*
- adobe: *medium brown or camel color*
- jaspered brown: *mainly brown with some white fibers*
- red mesa: *copper/reddish-brown*
- rio grande: *deep brown/black*
- sombra: *a light color in between gray and brown*
- mesa: *brown*
- pearl: *mainly white with some black or cream fibers*
- silver: *light gray*
- blue: *light gray with blue overtones*
- storm: *dark gray*
- jaspered black: *mainly black with some white fibers*
- jet: *black with no white and little or no brown fibers*

KNITTING NEEDLE CONVERSION CHART

KNITTING NEEDLES

U.S.	METRIC
0	2mm
1	2.25mm
2	2.75mm
3	3.25mm
4	3.5mm
5	3.75mm
6	4mm
7	4.5mm
8	5mm
9	5.5mm
10	6mm
10 ½	6.5mm
11	8mm
13	9mm
15	10mm
17	12.75mm
19	15mm
35	19mm

A BRIEF SELECTION OF CHILDREN'S BOOKS FOR THOSE WHO **LOVE** YARN

- Extra Yarn
by Mac Barnett
- The Mitten
by Jan Brett
- Mr. Putter & Tabby Spin the Yarn
by Cynthia Rylant and Arthur Howard
- Shall I Knit You a Hat?
by Kate Klise
- Farmer Brown Shears His Sheep
by Terri Sloat
- Phoebe's Sweater
by Joanna Johnson
- Derek the Knitting Dinosaur
by Mary Blackwood
- Woolbur
by Leslie Helakoski
- Hank and Gracie Save the Day
by Stacy Klaus
- From Sheep to Sweater
by Robin Nelson
- Sheep in a Jeep
by Nancy Shaw
- Knitting Nell
by Julie Jersild Roth

{ If you are wondering whether or not you've got enough yarn left to finish a row when coming to the end of a skein, measure the remaining yarn. If it's four or more times the width of the row you're knitting, you should have enough. }

Historically, war has caused patriotic themes to find their way into all sorts of pop culture, including music. During the first and second World Wars, songs were used to buoy spirits and remind soldiers and their families of better times to come. Patriotic songs thus glossed over the brutal and bloody aspects of war, focusing on optimistic calls to action, idealized images of the folks back home, and wistful songs of love and longing. One subgenre of patriotic wartime music was the knitting song: pop songs intended to motivate those at home to produce knitted goods that would help warm and clothe soldiers serving abroad. Examples include "Knitting" by Muriel Bruce and Baron Aliotti (1915) (sample lyric: "Knitting with a smile, knitting with a sigh, for their sons and brothers, fathers, lovers, too"); "Pick Up Your Knitting" by Dudley Brill and Norman R. Finch (1941); "There's a Girl Who Is Knitting for You" by George Hopkins and Florence Mills Nixson (1918); and "Listen to the Knocking at the Knitting Club" by Bert Hanlon and Harry VonTilzer (1917).

WHAT 1980s TOY TREND WAS IMMORTALIZED IN A *VOGUE KNITTING* PATTERN FEATURE?

▶ *Cabbage Patch Kids.*

The Fall/Winter 1985 *Vogue Knitting* featured matching clothing patterns for both girl and doll: a stylish snowflake ski sweater, an Aran cardi with matching hat, and a cardigan/vest/skirt/tam combo.

◆ ◆ ◆ ◆

NEW ZEALAND AND AUSTRALIA

have the highest lamb and mutton consumption rate per capita at 50 pounds per year for New Zealand and 37 pounds per year for Australia. (Compare that with the US rate of 1 pound per capita, per year.)

◆ ◆ ◆ ◆

In late 18th-century England, the so-called Luddite riots began as workers, fearing their livelihoods, protested the implementation of various types of industrial machinery. In October 1779, for example, spinners and weavers yelling, "Men! Not machines!" broke all the spinning mules and frames they could find to protest increasing mechanization in English towns like Bolton, Chorley, and Blackburn.

DO YOU HAVE TROUBLE FOLLOWING
KNITTING CHARTS?
TRY ONE OF THESE HANDY FIXES

• Use sticky notes or removable highlighter tape to mark rows as you go.

• Write each row on a separate index card, punch a hole in the corners, and use a ring binder to hold them together in the proper order. Flip the card as you work each row.

• Use highlighter markers to color-code the boxes on the chart. For example, color all yarn over boxes yellow, color all k2tog boxes pink, color all ssk boxes blue, etc.

• Use a metal stand and flat magnetic strips to mark the row you're on.

Have you ever wondered what it would be like to see the world through a goat's eyes?

Now, with a computer game called Goat Simulator, you can. Well, sort of. Released in April 2014 by a gaming company called Coffee Stain Studios, Goat Simulator allows a player to control a female goat. The goat can complete tasks or tricks, such as jumping and running, bouncing on trampolines, licking or running to objects, and other goatlike behavior. Small golden goat statues are hidden throughout the environment, and collecting them allows the player to change from a goat to, say, a giraffe, while hidden "Easter eggs" reveal surprises like a goat jet pack. The creators have already received a complaint from a farmer who didn't like that the goat got knocked around in the game, although developer Armin Ibrisagic is quick to note that the goat is never injured: "The goat could be an inspiration to all of us. No matter what happens, you pick yourself up and start over."

Scientists estimate that approximately 8 percent of rams **seek to mate** exclusively with other rams instead of with ewes.

The term *argyle,*

originally spelled *argyll,*
and the pattern we associate with
the term (a checkerboard-like
pattern set on a diagonal, with
lines running through it) dates
back to 16th-century Scotland.
Argyll is a county in Scotland
ruled by Clan Campbell. The
argyle pattern may have been an
attempt to replicate an intricate
tartan pattern for hose to be
worn with kilts by using a more
simplified form. The Scottish
knitwear company Pringle
of Scotland is credited with
popularizing the argyle pattern
in the 1920s. England's Duke of
Windsor was seen wearing argyle
socks both on and off the golf
course, and eventually American manufacturers like Brooks Brothers
began producing argyle knitwear of their own. Today, the argyle pattern
is indelibly associated with golf and all things preppy.

Color Key

□ white

■ black

■ grey

■ pink

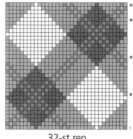

32-st rep

❖   ❖   ❖   ❖   ❖

One of the most famous photographs of Gandhi

was taken by photographer Margaret Bourke-White in 1946 for
Life magazine. The iconic photograph shows Gandhi sitting by his
spinning wheel. *Life*'s notes for the photo shoot state that Gandhi

*spins every day for 1 hr. beginning usually at 4. All members of his
ashram must spin. He and his followers encourage everyone to spin.
Even M. B-W was encouraged to lay [aside] her camera to spin.*

In 2013, a charkha spinning wheel used by Gandhi when he
was imprisoned during the 1920s sold for a whopping
110,000 pounds at a UK auction.

SURNAMES DERIVED
FROM FIBER-Y OCCUPATIONS

NAME	HERITAGE	MEANING
BERGER	*Norman French*	shepherd
BISSET	*French*	fine linen, probably referring to a weaver
BRODEUR	*French*	embroiderer
BURRELL	*English*	type of cloth; probably referred to one who sold it
CAUSER	*French*	probably derived from the word for leggings and referred to one who made and sold them
DEXTER	*Old English*	dyer
DRAPER	*English*	one who makes and sells woolen cloth
FÄRBER	*German*	dyer; from *farbe*, meaning color
FULLER	*English*	one who softened and cleaned woolen fabric
GULYÁS	*Hungarian*	herdsman or stockman
HOWARD	*Old English*	from *ewehirder*, meaning one who herds ewes
KADLEC	*Czech*	weaver
KNOPF	*German*	button maker or button seller
KOZIOL	*Polish*	goat, probably goat herder

NAME	HERITAGE	MEANING
KUNKEL	*German*	maker of spindles
LANE	*French*	from *laine*, or wool; one working in wool trade
METAXAS	*Greek*	one who deals with silk
MONDADORI	*Italian*	one who chose the best fleeces to be made into wool
PECORA	*Italian*	flock, a shepherd
SCHÄFER	*German*	shepherd
SCHEER	*German*	shearer or cutter; used for both barbers and tailors
SHEPARD	*English*	shepherd
SHERMAN	*English*	one who used shears, as a sheep-shearer
TAKÁCS	*Hungarian*	weaver
TUCKER	*Old English*	one who fulls cloth
WALKER	*English*	one who walked on cloth to thicken it
WEBB, WEBSTER	*English*	weaver

The Worcestershire and Sherwood Foresters Regiment of the British Army adopted a ram as its mascot in 1858.

The regiment captured a ram at the Siege of Kotah. It then marched nearly 3,000 miles along with the soldiers through central India. Named Private Derby, the original mascot died in 1863; however, the regiment still continued to adopt a ram as mascot.

In the early 20th century, a tradition was started in which the Duke of Devonshire presents the regiment with a Swaledale ram selected from his own flock. The mascot is always named Private Derby, has his own regimental number, and receives his own rations.

Private Derby is issued two handlers who accompany him and care for him; the senior handler has the title Ram Major, while the junior is known as the Ram Orderly. While on parade, Private Derby wears a red coat with green and gold facings.

MARY ROWLANDSON (1637–1711) was an American colonist who was captured by a raiding party of Native Americans during the conflict called King Philip's War. For more than 11 weeks, Rowlandson and her three children (one of whom died in captivity) were forced to accompany their captors as they attempted to elude pursuers. Rowlandson took her knitting needles with her and was able to barter her skills in creating clothing to obtain better treatment, including badly needed food and clothing; at one point she traded a pair of knit stockings for a quart of peas, and on another occasion she received a hat and silk handkerchief in exchange for three pairs of stockings.

How many horns does a sheep have? It depends.

■ ■ ■ ■ Some sheep are naturally hornless, or *polled*. In some breeds, the male has horns, while the female does not. In other breeds, both sheep have horns, and in still others, certain strains of the breed are horned while others are polled. A Rocky Mountain Bighorn sheep may have horns that weigh as much as 30 pounds. The Jacob breed typically grows four horns (but may have two or six horns), and the Desert Dragon breed may have three horns.

●●● MAMMALIAN MATH

male alpaca + female llama = **huarizo**

female alpaca + male llama = **misti or misto**

male vicuña + female alpaca = **vicuña-paco**

female vicuña + male alpaca = **paco-vicuña**

llama female + camel male = **cama**

buffalo (American bison) + Tibetan yak = **yakalo**

buffalo + domestic cattle = **beefalo and cattalo**

yak + domestic cow = **dzo**

sheep + goat = **geep**

SOME OF THESE CROSS-BREEDS ARE
MORE COMMON THAN OTHERS.
*For example, given that sheep and goats belong
to different genuses, cross-breeding the two
is rare and offspring are usually stillborn. And
due to the, er, logistical difficulties of mating
when animals are of very different sizes,
some of these hybrids must be created through
artificial insemination.*

Knitters in some areas of the
world tension their yarn by **winding
the yarn around their necks.**
The ball of yarn is placed lower than the body,
with the yarn wrapped around the back of the
neck (or through a pin or around a button at
the front of the knitter's clothing).
The yarn tensions itself, without additional
wrapping or pulling. This method of
tensioning the yarn is associated with various
Mediterranean countries and is variously called
Portuguese, Andean, Greek, Turkish, and/or
Macedonian knitting.

US STATE
THAT GROWS
THE MOST
COTTON:
➤ Texas

*Other US states
that grow cotton:*
• Alabama
• Arkansas
• Arizona
• California
• Florida
• Georgia
• Kansas
• Louisiana
• Mississippi
• Missouri
• New Mexico
• North Carolina
• Oklahoma
• South Carolina
• Tennessee
• Virginia

*Country that
grows the
most cotton:*
➤ China

• India and the
United States are
the second and
third runners-up,
respectively.

MATCH THE DISEASE TO THE FIBER PRODUCER THAT MAY GET IT

1. mycoplasma haemolamae

2. snuffles

3. psylosis

4. Cache Valley virus

5. caprine arthritis encephalitis syndrome

6. grasserie

7. scrapie

8. malignant catarrhal fever

9. mosaic virus

· · · · · · · · · ·

SHEEP
BISON
SILKWORMS
BAMBOO
RABBITS
ALPACAS & LLAMAS
COTTON
SHEEP & GOATS
GOATS

CORRECT ANSWERS

1. alpacas & llamas;
2. rabbits; 3. cotton;
4. sheep; 5. goats;
6. silkworms;
7. sheep & goats;
8. bison; 9. bamboo

Sericulture, the production of silk,

was so important to Chinese culture that it has been estimated that 230 of the 5,000 most common Chinese written characters contain the character for silk as a component.

The American Livestock Breeds Conservancy, a nonprofit group devoted to genetic conservation and preservation of heritage breeds of livestock and poultry, placed six breeds of American sheep on its most recent critical list. The "critical" designation means that fewer than 200 animals of that breed were registered in the United States, and fewer than 2,000 of that breed are estimated in the world. The 2013 list of critical US sheep breeds consisted of the Romeldale/CVM, Florida Cracker, Gulf Coast/Gulf Coast Native, Hog Island, Leicester Longwool and Santa Cruz breeds.

Knitting Namesakes

HAVE AN URGE TO NAME YOUR CHILD
(WHETHER HUMAN OR FURRY) SOMETHING
FIBER-RELATED? CHOICES ABOUND:

■ Honor one of the grande dames of knitting by opting for *Elizabeth* (as in Zimmermann), *Barbara* (as in Walker), *Cornelia* (as in Mee, who wrote some of the first knitting pattern booklets), *Mary* (as in Thomas), *Alice* (as in Starmore) or *Debbie* (as in Bliss).

■ Look no further than the name of your favorite yarn company. Who wouldn't love a little ROWAN, PATON, ANZULA, KOIGU, LOTUS, OPAL, or ZEALANA running around? Having boy-girl twins? No worries—how about SPUD AND CHLOE?

■ Give your lamb a name that means lamb: Oona, Talia, Rachelle, Cordero, Agnes, Karitsa, Hamal, or Ovid.

■ Let a popular pattern inspire you. You probably don't want to name your child *Clapotis* or *Hitchhiker*, but there's always *Ishbel, Annis, Hedera, Haruni,* or *Petal.*

SHETLAND WOOL TERMS

• **lemmen:** combed wool from Shetland sheep for spinning

• **macking:** knitting

• **single macking:** flat knitting

• **plain macking:** stockinette stitch

• **reggies:** garter stitch

• **right loop:** knit stitch

In the 14th century, King Edward III decreed that the Speaker of the House of Lords of Parliament should sit on a bale of wool, now called the "Woolsack," in order to symbolize the importance of the wool trade to England's economy. The Lord Speaker still sits on a seat stuffed with wool and covered with red cloth.

⋙→ A SELECTION OF SPORTS TEAMS
WITH FIBER-RELATED TEAM NAMES

■ ST. LOUIS RAMS
USA; football

■ BOSTON RED SOX
USA; baseball

■ CHICAGO WHITE SOX
USA; baseball

■ UNIVERSITY OF ARKANSAS
AT MONTICELLO
USA; men's sports—the BOLL
WEEVILS, women's sports—the
COTTON BLOSSOMS

■ BUCKNELL
COLLEGE BISON
USA; college athletics

■ UNIVERSITY OF
COLORADO BUFFALOES
USA; college athletics

■ CONNECTICUT
COLLEGE CAMELS
USA; college athletics

■ BLUE MOUNTAIN
STATE COLLEGE GOATS
Pennsylvania, USA; college
athletics

■ BARD COLLEGE AT
SIMON'S ROCK LLAMAS
Massachusetts, USA;
college athletics

■ STEINBÖCKE (mountain goat)
Austria; Rugby Union National
team

■ MOUFFLONS (wild horned
sheep) Cypress; Rugby Union
National team

■ RABBITOHS;
South Sydney, Australia;
Australia professional
rugby team

■ DIZZY LLAMAS
Boston, Massachusetts, USA;
athletic club

■ FLORIDA
FIGHTING POSSUMS
USA; lacrosse club

■ VICKY THE VICUÑA
Official mascot of 2005
FIFA under-17 soccer world
championship

  The film *THE DARK KNIGHT RISES* includes an "Easter egg" reference to Dickens's *A Tale of Two Cities*. Dark Knight archvillain Bane is shown knitting, drawing parallels between him and Dickens's infamous Madame Defarge. Warner Brothers reportedly confirmed the connection, but declined to comment on it.

CELEBRITY KNITTERS
Present Day

Ryan Gosling	Felicity Huffman	Paulina Porizkova
Julia Roberts	Tracey Ullman	Kristin Davis
Catherine Zeta-Jones	David Arquette	Geri Halliwell
Christina Hendricks	Amanda Seyfried	Cindy Crawford
Karen Allen	Kate Moss	Katherine Heigl
Darryl Hannah	Vanna White	Kate, the Duchess of Cambridge
Dakota Fanning	Deborah Norville	
	Meryl Streep	

Rose Warfman is known as a Holocaust survivor and heroine of the French Resistance during World War II.

Warfman survived imprisonment at several Nazi concentration camps, including Auschwitz. At Birkenau, she was among a group of women assigned the task of knitting undershirts for German infants. Later, when cold weather arrived, the women were told to knit socks for German soldiers. As an act of passive resistance, Warfman reportedly created large knots in the bottoms of the socks to render them unusable. ⁓

The wool rinse EUCALAN got its name by combining the names of two of the products in the original formula: *eucalyptus and lanolin.*

RHYMES USED TO TEACH
Children How To Knit

ENGLISH STYLE
OF KNITTING
In through the front door,
Run around the back.
Down through the window,
And off jumps Jack.

Into the bunny hole,
Run around the tree.
Out of the bunny hole,
Away runs he.

Jack goes in,
Puts on his scarf,
Comes back out,
And takes it off.

Needle to needle and stitch to stitch,
Pull the old woman out of the ditch.
If you ain't out by the time I'm in,
I'll rap your knuckles with
my knitting pin.

PURLING
Down through the bunny hole,
Around the big tree,
Up pops the bunny,
And off goes she!

Under the fence
Catch the sheep
Back you go
Off you leap.

CONTINENTAL STYLE
OF KNITTING
In through the front door,
Up over the back,
Peek through the window,
And off jumps Jack!

SOCK KNITTING
To knit a stocking, needles four,
cast on three needles and no more,
each needle stitches eight and twenty,
then one for seam stitch will be plenty.

1n 1967, a fleece-to-garment competition was held as part of a promotional event seeking to highlight the wool trade in Wairoa, a town on the North Island of New Zealand.

During Wairoa Wool Week, two teams sought to break the world record for the amount of time it took to turn a freshly shorn fleece into an adult-size sweater. The first team of 12 women sat in the window of a furniture shop with their spinning wheels. It took them 7 hours, 21 minutes, and 25 seconds to spin, ply, then knit a man's sweater—a world record at the time. The second team consisted of 12 women from the Maori tribe. Although they did not use any machines—the sheep was shorn with hand blades, and instead of using wheels, the women hand-rolled the fiber into yarn—it only took the Maori women an hour longer than the team using spinning wheels.

➤ MULE-SPUN YARN has nothing to do with the offspring of a male donkey and female horse, but rather refers to the spinning mule machinery invented in the late 1770s by Englishman Samuel Compton. Compton did not have the financial resources necessary to immediately develop his invention, playing his homemade violin for pennies at the local theater to support himself while he perfected it. Although the spinning mule became wildly popular, Compton's inability to secure a patent meant that he earned next to nothing despite his ingenuity.

TYPE OF SWEDISH ETHNIC SWEATER OR PRODUCT FROM IKEA?

Ullared	Fana
JANSJÖ	ALMSTED
Delsbo	**Spede**
Bjarbo	SKOGABY
OLTEDAL	DJURSPÄR

Key: **Bold** *are sweaters;* ALL CAPS *are Ikea products.*

In the Old Testament's Song of Solomon, David compares his lover's teeth to a flock of sheep:
"Thy teeth are like a flock of sheep that are even shorn, which came up from the washing; whereof every one bear twins, and none is barren among them."

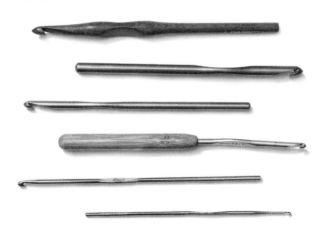

⫸ SOME TYPES OF CROCHET

Tunisian crochet creates a very symmetric and squared-off set of stitches that almost look woven. Worked on a tool that looks like a combination of a knitting needle and crochet hook, this technique involves creating stitches in two steps without turning the work. After a row of chains is made, the first step involves drawing a loop through each chain in the row, skipping the first one as is normally done in regular crochet. This leaves a row of live stitches on the hook, instead of just a single one. The second step generally requires the crocheter to wrap the yarn over the hook and draw it through two loops at a time, reducing the number of stitches one by one (not unlike a knitted bind-off). Tunisian crochet is also called Afghan crochet or Afghan stitch, *tricot écossais* (Scottish knitting), shepherd's knitting, hook knitting, and railroad knitting.

Broomstick lace (also called jiffy lace) is a very airy fabric with large loops that slant to one side and are fastened with crochet stitches. Broomstick lace is made with a regular crochet hook (selected based on the weight of the yarn) along with a very large knitting needle or other large tube like, well, a broomstick! The diameter of the broomstick or knitting needle determines the size of the loops. After chaining a row, the crocheter draws a loop through each chain and places it on the broomstick. After all the loops are made, the crocheter draws the yarn through groups of loops and fastens them off.

Filet crochet is a term that was widely used in the 19th century to refer to crochet patterns that copied the look of lace. Filet crochet tends to be made with very fine mercerized cotton in mesh patterns, often with central motifs, using only two stitches: chains and double crochets.

Hairpin lace, or hairpin crochet, is made on a special tool called a hairpin fork, loom, or staple. The tool contains two prongs set parallel to each other, and the maker creates stripes by winding yarn around the prongs and fastening the loops with crochet stitches, forming a sort of spine. The strips are then joined together with traditional crochet stitches.

Irish crochet, or Irish lace, is a style of crochet that became widespread in the famine years in Ireland. It provided a means for impoverished Irish girls and women to earn money by crocheting elaborate lace patterns, often inspired by the tatted lace of Continental Europe. Using small hooks and extremely fine yarn, motifs are worked individually then joined, with meshlike or chained backgrounds in between motifs. During its heyday, crocheters would create their own unique patterns and motifs and guard them jealously from other crocheters. However, the rise of industrialization made it impossible for hand-crocheted lace to compete with machine-made lace, and the technique lost popularity in the 20th century. ✳

☛ The type of hat known as a BALACLAVA was named after the Battle of Balaclava, fought during the Crimean War in 1854. A balaclava is a hat that exposes only part of the face, sometimes only the eyes or eyes/nose/mouth. Balaclavas were sent to British soldiers to help protect them from the cold. Today balaclavas are perhaps more closely associated with bank robbers.

Prior to the 17th century, the MERINO industry was so important in Spain that EXPORTING A MERINO SHEEP was an offense punishable by death.

◆ ◆ ◆ ◆ ◆

⟫⟶ FAVORITE
Elizabeth Zimmermann Quotes

"Most people have an obsession; mine is knitting."
– KNITTING WITHOUT TEARS

"Really, all you need to become a good knitter
are wool, needles, hands, and slightly below-average intelligence.
Of course, superior intelligence,
such as yours and mine, is an advantage."
– KNITTING WITHOUT TEARS

"[T]here are few knitting problems that will not yield to a blend of
common sense, ingenuity, and resourcefulness."
– THE OPINIONATED KNITTER

"Having observed young people for a couple of generations,
and seen them go through all manner of fashion-tortures
without batting an eye, right down to the current exposure of bare blue
shivering shanks in winter, I know that they can and will endure all
manner of discomfort in order to wear what they want to wear."
– KNITTER'S ALMANAC

"Properly practiced, knitting soothes the troubled spirit,
and it doesn't hurt the untroubled spirit either."
– KNITTING WITHOUT TEARS

"Change colors if and when the spirit moves you."
– KNITTER'S ALMANAC

"Tight knitters lead a hard and anxious life. They grab needles
and wool so tightly that great strain is put upon their hand muscles,
nay, arm, shoulder, and even neck muscles, in extreme cases.
They must let go of everything from time to time, just to rest,
and then resume knitting, with what looks like a careworn expression,
although they neither admit, nor, in most cases, believe this.
The tight little stitches they make must be forced along their (right)
needle, and more tight little stitches force up
along their (left) needle, to be squeezed in their turn."
– KNITTING WITHOUT TEARS

"I know that spinning sets me in a trance; it soothes me and charges my batteries at the same time. When times are tough I sit down to spin during the news-broadcasts, with therapeutic results."
– *KNITTER'S ALMANAC*

"Soft wool from the simple silly sheep can be as fine as a cobweb, tough and strong as string, or light and soft as down. There are scientific reasons why wool is the best material for knitting, and into these I will not go. I only know that it is warm, beautiful, and durable."
– *KNITTING WITHOUT TEARS*

If the reader is unfamiliar with Elizabeth Zimmermann, she should IMMEDIATELY seek to remedy this deficiency with a trip to the local bookshop or library. Known as **"EZ"** to her legions of fans, Zimmermann wrote several iconic books about knitting, beloved both for their commonsense, rational approach to the craft and for her often-humorous, conversational, and witty writing style. ✳

❖ The character Anna Makarovna from Leo Tolstoy's 1869 novel *War and Peace* is described as having created a unique method of knitting socks two at a time, one inside the other:

This meant two stockings, which by a secret process known only to herself Anna Makarovna used to knit at the same time on the same needles, and which, when they were ready, she always triumphantly drew, one out of the other, in the children's presence.

Today, you can learn the "secret process" that Anna used with a simple Google search.

The bimonthly *Sheep!* magazine bills itself as *"the voice of the independent flockmaster."*

From roughly the 12th to 16th centuries, the arts and trades in Florence were controlled by secular corporations called guilds.

Guilds helped organize the city's economic life, prevented competition from nonmembers, provided training and social services for members, and ensured the quality of the members' work. One of the most powerful guilds in Florence was the Arte della Lana, the wool guild. The Arte della Lana oversaw the weaving of woolen cloth and had the exclusive right to import raw wool, then weave and dye it. A rival guild, the Arte di Calimala, had the exclusive right to import already-woven cloth and finish it through methods such as fulling or a process called calendaring.

The guilds of Florence declined with the rise of mercantilism and eventually were replaced by other administrative bodies. ✳

Emblem of Arte della Lana ☞

◻ **Yarn that is "dyed in the wool"** is dyed before the wool (or other fiber) is actually spun into yarn. Also called *stock dyed* or *fleece dyed*, the constituent fibers are dyed, then blended and spun. Yarn may be dyed in the wool in order to achieve heathered color effects. For example, a mill may dye some fiber pink and some fiber blue, then blend them together and spin them into a yarn that reads as a heathered purple. Or, the process can be used to create stripes, as it is with Noro yarns, which are made of fibers dyed in the wool then spun in sequence to create stripes that slowly blend from one color to the next.

{ **Great Britain** has more than 60 native breeds of sheep. }

Why is the most unsavory or despised member of the family called the black sheep?

No one really knows for sure, but one explanation is that black wool cannot be dyed and is therefore worth less. So a shepherd or wool merchant would regard the black sheep as worth less than lighter ones. Another possibility stems from the fact that the color black was viewed as a mark of the devil in old England. (Animal shelters today still report that black dogs and cats are harder to adopt than other colors.) Still another source suggests that the idiom *black sheep* is derived from a misinterpretation or mistranslation of a passage from the Old Testament in which Jacob offers to take only dark and multicolored sheep, leaving his master with all-white sheep to make it easy to tell if any had been stolen. On the other hand, black sheep weren't universally regarded as a bad thing: sources say that shepherds in certain parts of England viewed a black sheep as good luck. Interestingly, the idiom *black sheep* is also used in several other languages; in Russian, the phrase *white crow* plays a similar role.

IN 1951, TWO MEN DIGGING FOR PEAT DISCOVERED HUMAN REMAINS IN A REMOTE PART OF SHETLAND. ARCHEOLOGISTS DETERMINED THAT THE REMAINS WERE MALE AND WERE BURIED AROUND 1700.

The remains were dubbed Gunnister Man, after the location where they were discovered. Textile historians were particularly pleased to see that Gunnister Man's clothing was largely intact, preserved by his bed of peat. Gunnister Man was clad in a suit made of fulled twill, and his shirt and outer jacket were also made of wool. But it was his accessories that fascinated the knitters of the world. Gunnister Man had two white wool caps, one with a turned-up brim and one with a plain brim, both knit mainly in stockinette stitch; long gauntlets made of white wool that had been fulled; and white wool stockings that reached above his knees, with decreases lined up along a faux seam in the back. The feet of his stockings had been resoled, while the legs were in fairly good shape. The fanciest item, remaining relatively intact, was a small purse knitted in gray yarn with a ribbed top and three bands of patterning (one white, two red) decorated by tassels. ⬿

Knitting historian GWYN MORGAN notes that
MOST TRADITIONAL GUERNSEY SWEATERS feature sleeves
worked by picking up stitches around the shoulder and working
down—which means that if the sleeves get damaged or excessively
worn, the knitter can repair them by unraveling from the cuff.

The camel hair used in knitting yarns comes from the Bactrian camel, a two-humped domesticated species called Camelus bactrianus.

The one-humped camel, or dromedary, is a distinct
species not used for its fiber.

AUGUST FERDINAND MÖBIUS WAS A GERMAN
ASTRONOMER AND MATHEMATICIAN
WHO LIVED FROM 1790 TO 1868.

(He also happened to be a distant descendant of Martin Luther.)

One of Möbius's best-known discoveries is the strip or loop
that bears his name. Take a narrow piece of paper and make a loop.
Give the loop a half twist, then join the ends. The resulting shape
is of great interest to mathematicians due to its unique properties,
but it's **also of great interest to knitters**, who quickly adopted
the Möbius strip to make cowls—the half twist that is knit in
helps keep the cowl flat under a jacket. In addition, one end of the
Möbius can be worn around the neck as a scarf while the
other covers the head like a monk's hood.

A bellwether is a trendsetter or leader;
the term comes from the Middle English *bellewether*, which refers
to the placing of a bell around the neck of a castrated sheep
(called a *wether*). By listening to the bell, the movement of the
entire flock could be determined.

ACTUAL KNITTING VANITY PLATES

LUV2KNIT

1MOREROW

BUY YARN

KNITSOX

YRNJNKY

P2TOG

YO K2TOG

KNIT ON

EWEANDI

HNDKNTR

LOPI

Who was the first living textile artist to have a one-man show at the Victoria and Albert Museum in London?

KAFFE FASSETT.

If you're one of those
knitters
who hates to purl,
you're not alone.
Some textile historians have opined that the purl stitch was developed much later, perhaps hundreds of years later, than the knit stitch. One source suggests that the first surviving purl stitches in a knitted artifact date from the mid-1500s, well after knitting was under way in various countries around the world.

☞ STEP ASIDE, PAUL THE OCTOPUS.

Sonny Wool is the new oracle in town. A sheep from the North Island of New Zealand, Sonny Wool is known for his excellent record of predicting the winner of the New Zealand national rugby team's matches during the 2011 World Cup. How does a sheep predict the winner of a rugby match? Well, Sonny Wool is presented with two boxes of hay, each labeled with the name of one of the competing teams. His handlers note which box he eats from first and interpret this as his selection. Skeptics, please note that Sonny Wool correctly predicted 7 out of 10 results in the 2011 World Cup—not too shabby! Sonny has his own agent, Facebook page, and Twitter account, naturally.

Queen Mary, wife of England's King George V, knitted a pair of socks for a soldier in World War I; her patriotic example was intended to inspire other knitters to produce knitted goods to clothe English soldiers. The socks were sold at auction to benefit the Red Cross and were purchased by Sir Hugh Macdonald, who was the premier of Manitoba, Canada. The Macdonalds sent the socks to a Winnipeg soldier serving on the front, but he was killed in action, probably before he could wear them. The socks ended up on display in Alberta's Glenbow Museum, where they can be seen today.

MATCH THE **HISTORIC** KNITTING TERM WITH THE **CURRENT** NAME FOR THE STITCH

1. Spotted knitting
2. Hit and Miss
3. All Fool's Welt
4. Seam
5. Patti knitting
6. Knit and Seam
7. Patent knitting

A. Single ribbing
B. Blackberry stitch
C. Brioche stitch
D. Ribbing
E. 7 rows of garter stitch plus 1 purled row
F. Trinity stitch
G. Purl stitch

KEY: **1.** F; **2.** A; **3.** E; **4.** G; **5.** B; **6.** D; **7.** C

WORDS

USED TO DESCRIBE HUMAN BEHAVIOR DERIVED FROM OVINE BEHAVIOR

to ram into something:
to butt or beat at something, as when a male sheep head-butts as a sign of aggression

to flock:
to gather together in a group, as sheep do; also used as a noun to describe a group of people organized under a leader, as a sheep follow their shepherd

a herd:
a large group of people; "the herd" is sometimes used to mean the masses

to graze:
to eat lightly in small amounts throughout the day, as a sheep grazes on grass

a lamb:
a young, foolish, or weak person

Godey's Lady's Book was an American magazine aimed at women that was wildly popular in the mid-19th century.

☛ The magazine included fashion plates, dressmaking patterns, fiction and poetry, sheet music, and a variety of needlework patterns. Knitting patterns might include garters, collars and cuffs, petticoats, shawls, hats and hoods, purses, and novelty items. By 1850, *Godey's Lady's Book* had 150,000 subscribers; it was sold in 1877 and ceased publication in 1898. *Godey's* is especially noteworthy because its publisher began copyrighting its contents in 1845, at a time when other publishers did not do so. *Godey's* longest-serving editor, Sarah Josepha Hale (who, incidentally, wrote the song "Mary Had a Little Lamb") favored publishing original American manuscripts, devoted three special issues to work produced only by women, and regularly devoted space in the magazine to discussing women in the workforce.

KNITTED SACK.

KNITTED PARISIAN SPENCER.

KRAEMER YARNS, once known as **Kraemer Textiles**, is one of the oldest remaining textile mills still operating in the United States.

The company was started by Henry Kraemer in 1887 as a manufacturer of women's hosiery; in 1907, the company was purchased by the Schmidt family but retained the Kraemer name. Today the mill operates 24 hours a day, seven days a week, spinning about 20,000 pounds of yarn each week—enough yarn to go around the globe 1.5 times.

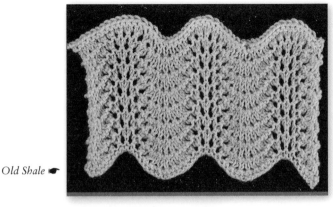

Old Shale ☛

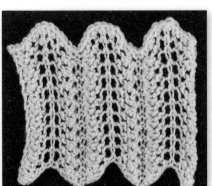

☚ Feather & Fan

What's the difference—*or is there one*—between Feather & Fan and Old Shale?

I n recent years, the terms have become intermingled, and even a quick Internet search reveals much confusion between the two traditional stitch patterns. Shetland lace experts SHARON MILLER and ELIZABETH LOVICK agree, however, that the terms refer to distinct, albeit related, pattern stitches. Feather & Fan (Mary Thomas refers to it as simply "Feather Stitch") features pairs of eyelets in columns; the eyelets in Old Shale form curving lines instead of straight columns. There are other differences, depending on the specific variation being used: Feather & Fan generally has a two-row repeat, whereas Old Shale has a four-row repeat. The names given to these commonly used stitch patterns reflect the tendency to name patterns based on what they resemble. As Lovick, Miller, and others have pointed out, the rows of decreases in Feather & Fan resemble the center of a feather, while the eyelets look to some like a fan. Old Shale may be derived from "Old Shell," as the curving lines of the eyelets in this pattern mirror the shape of a clam shell; Shetland experts note that "shale" may be the way "shell" sounds when pronounced in the Shetland dialect. ✳

The instantly recognizable **SEAL OF COTTON** was created in 1973 by an ad agency in San Francisco—the same ad agency that designed such iconic trademarks as the Coca-Cola logo and the patch sewn on Levi's jeans.

The enterprising Dukes Wooters, who was president of Cotton Incorporated (a trade group for American cotton growers), decided that cotton needed a brand identity so that it would be regarded as a desirable consumer item rather than a humdrum agricultural product. Cotton Incorporated's promotional efforts were so successful that an estimated 8 out of 10 consumers today recognize the logo.

A SELECTION OF MOVIE AND TELEVISION CHARACTERS

WHO KNIT

Morticia Addams (*The Addams Family*)

Mrs. Weasley (the Harry Potter movie series)

Pingu (claymation children's television series from Switzerland)

Liz Lemon (*30 Rock*; every year she takes up knitting for a week)

Lucy and Ethel (*I Love Lucy*)

Izzie Stevens (*Grey's Anatomy*)

Gromit (*Wallace & Gromit*)

Babs (*Chicken Run*)

Holly Golightly (*Breakfast at Tiffany's*)

THE STORY OF BOHUS KNITTING
IS THE STORY OF A SUCCESSFUL COTTAGE INDUSTRY
THAT ENDURED FOR DECADES.

During the economic depression of the 1930s and 1940s, an Austrian-born woman named Emma Jacobsson, who was married to the governor of the Bohuslän province of Sweden, was approached by a group of local women asking for help in beginning some type of home-based industry. The depression had hit this part of Sweden particularly hard, and the women sought a way to supplement their families' incomes from their homes so they could bring in money while still caring for their family and farms. Initially, the group began crafting Christmas ornaments, but this provided only seasonal income, and the women needed more. The women briefly tried making stuffed animals, but this

didn't work out. Finally, they decided to try handknitting. The Bohuslän region did not have a strong regional knitting tradition, unlike other areas of Sweden, so the women decided to create their own.

VISITORS TO WALES CAN PARTICIPATE IN AN ACTIVITY CALLED SHEEP TREKKING.

Participants select one of the specially trained Jacob sheep and lead it on a leash for a two-and-a-half-hour hike toward the Black Mountains. The sheep are outfitted with special halters that allow them to carry a light lunch.

"Little Lamb who made thee
Dost thou know who made thee
Gave thee life & bid thee feed.
By the stream & o'er the mead;
Gave thee clothing of delight,
Softest clothing wooly bright;"

– WILLIAM BLAKE

● ● ●

IN THE SECOND HALF OF THE 19TH CENTURY, bone crochet hooks were fashioned from baleen, or whalebone, as well as from the shin bones of cows. By the turn of the century, baleen became scarce and only cow bones were used. By the late 1920s, cows were being butchered at an earlier age than they previously were in the United States, and their shin bones were too short for making crochet hooks. Cow bone was then imported from Argentina, where cows lived longer, until the development of plastic made the use of bone obsolete.

NUPP AND NEPP: are they the same or different?

DEFINITELY DIFFERENT.

• A *nepp* is a small bit of fiber that's added during the spinning process to create a little raised dot of color and texture. It's thought that nepps were first added accidentally, when a small amount of fiber of another color got mixed in with yarn being spun. The effect was pleasing, and so spinners began to deliberately add nepps to their yarn. You may also see nepps called *flecks* or *burrs*.

• *Nupp* is an Estonian word translated variously as "bud" or "button." It refers to a raised stitch, similar to a bobble, deliberately worked into a pattern by knitting multiple times in the same stitch then fastening off the extra loops. Nupps are frequently used in lace patterns, particularly those from Estonia and nearby regions.

■ ■ ■

LANOLIN, also called *wool grease* or *wool wax*, is a substance secreted by sheep to protect their wool and skin. After a sheep is shorn, the wool is washed with a special detergent to remove lanolin and other materials in the fleece. A centrifuge separates the lanolin from the other materials, and the lanolin is then used in products such as lipstick and moisturizer. Depending on factors like the breed and size of the sheep, lanolin makes up anywhere from 5 percent to 25 percent of the weight of a fleece.

After losing some 200 sheep to rustlers, a farmer in Devon, England, named John Heard used *nontoxic orange dye to dye all of his sheep traffic-cone orange.* Although the sheep look odd, his strategy works: thieves are reluctant to steal sheep that are so highly visible as to be easily identified.

In the 1920s and 1930s,
the Prince of Wales (later King Edward VIII, until he
abdicated and became the Duke of Windsor) was a
leading figure in men's fashion.

As *Men's Wear* magazine observed in 1924, "The average young man in America is more interested in the clothes of the Prince of Wales than in the clothes of any other individual on earth." The Windsor knot is named for him (although he preferred the four-in-hand knot); he adopted the use of zipped flies instead of buttons; he popularized the breeches called "plus fours" (they extended 4 inches below the knee); and he was daring in his use of color, pattern, and texture.

Knitters can thank the Prince of Wales for introducing the Fair Isle jumper to the masses when he famously wore one to play golf at St. Andrews in 1922. At the time, the sweater was incorrectly described as a souvenir of his visit to Japan or a gift from Romanian peasants, but the jumper was in fact made in the Shetland Islands using traditional Fair Isle-style

HRH The Prince of Wales,
painting by John Saint-Helier

patterns. The Prince only wore the sweater for an hour before changing into the obligatory red for dinner. But it is estimated that the knitters of the Shetland Isles earned an extra million dollars from the interest that the prince's one hour of wear generated in Fair Isle sweaters.

The first American man to have a design featured on the cover of *ROWAN* magazine was KAFFE FASSETT; the first American woman was AMY HERZOG.

How many knitting shops are there in the United States?

It depends on how you look at it. One trade organization estimated approximately 1,800 to 2,000 independent retailers (both brick-and-mortar and online) with at least half of their sales in yarn for 2013. This estimate includes shops that specialize in knitting and crochet as well as spinning and weaving, and it includes shops that also sell other needlework supplies. A 2013 trade industry directory contained listings for 688 stores specifically identifying themselves as specializing in only knitting supplies.

⫸→ A SELECTION OF MOVIES WITH DROOL-WORTHY HANDKNITS

The Big Lebowski

The Harry Potter series

The Hunger Games

The Santa Clause

Coraline

Twilight

The Holiday
(Cameron Diaz's cabled sweater)

The Hobbit

The Cider House Rules

Volver

My Super Ex-Girlfriend

☞ WRAPS PER INCH

The wraps per inch method is one way to obtain an approximation of a yarn's weight and gauge. Use a special tool made for this purpose or a standard wooden ruler. Attach the end of the yarn to the notch in the tool or tape it to the back of the ruler. Gently wrap a strand of the yarn around the tool or ruler to the 1-inch mark. Strands should be just touching but not overlapping. Count the number of wrapped strands that fit in an inch. Common measurements for yarn weights established by the Craft Yarn Council are as follows:

5 or fewer wraps per inch: Super Bulky (6)	9 to 11 wraps per inch: Worsted (4)	12 to 14 wraps per inch: DK to Sport Weight (2) (3)	15 to 18 wraps per inch: Fingering/Sock Weight (1)
6 to 8 wraps per inch: Bulky (5)		More than 18 wraps per inch: Lace Weight (0)	

➤ **New Zealand's Cairn Station, a farming area located on the South Island, has been home to Merino sheep since 1916. About 20 years ago, station sheep farmer Ben Aubrey began growing Pinot Gris grapes on the land.** When Aubrey was ready to turn the station's grapes into wine, he knew a strong brand was needed, so he hired consulting company Interbrand New Zealand to develop a brand identity. They created **Naked Sheep Wines** especially for Cairn Station, linking the area's long history of sheep shearing to its newer tradition of harvesting grapes. Each bottle is sold in a box made from native kahikatea wood from local fence posts; the boxes are designed with a pattern that blends images of Merino fiber with grapevine tendrils. The wine bottles are "naked"—they are clear and completely free of stickered labeling, with just a white sheep tag hanging from the top. Every 12th bottle is black and accompanied by a black sheep tag.

To be kept on tenterhooks means to keep someone in suspense.

The phrase—in use since at least the 1600s—has its origin in the making of **woolen cloth.** After cloth was woven, it still might contain vegetable matter, lanolin, and other undesirable materials, so the cloth needed to be washed to remove the impurities. To prevent the fabric from shrinking, it was stretched out over a large wooden frame called a tenter. The fabric was held in place by hooked nails attached at the selvedges called, yes, *tenterhooks.* Thus, a person is kept on tenterhooks when their emotions are figuratively stretched like cloth on a tenter.

☛ DK-WEIGHT YARN, CATEGORY 3
ON THE CRAFT YARN COUNCIL'S STANDARD YARN CHART, knits at approximately 5.5 stitches per inch, falling in between worsted weight yarn and sport weight yarn. Various explanations have been given for why the yarn is called *DK* or *double knitting* yarn. One anecdote suggests that during World War II, when wool was scarce and needed for military as well as domestic use, factories created a weight of yarn in between worsted and sport weight that could be used for either when knitting—so it would work in double the number of patterns. Another story suggests that the name derives from the fact that one strand of DK is equal to about two strands of fingering weight, making it doubly thick.

10

SHEEP BREEDS THAT YOU HAVEN'T HEARD OF . . .

but the wool of which you ought to be spinning with, as suggested by spinning expert/author Beth Shearer Smith:

POLYPAY

COLUMBIA

ROMNEY

TUNIS

ROMELDALE

TARGHEE

SUFFOLK

BORDER LEICESTER

TEESWATER

WENSLEYDALE

Author/designer **PRISCILLA GIBSON-ROBERTS** suggests using the wraps per inch measurement **as a way to estimate yardage for a plain, crewneck adult sweater, medium size.** Simply multiply the wraps per inch measurement by 100 for the estimated yardage.

IF YOUR SKEIN OF WOOL FEELS A BIT SCRATCHY, try giving it a bath in cool water plus a small amount of hair conditioner.

Hollywood actress Lana Turner was given the nickname **"the Sweater Girl"** after appearing in the 1937 film *They Won't Forget* wearing a tight-fitting blue wool sweater. The phrase "sweater girls" was also used to refer to the posters that American GIs displayed during World War II showing women—often actresses like Turner, Betty Grable, or Jane Russell—posing in tight-fitting sweaters. The armed forces encouraged the display of these posters, believing it would remind GIs of the country for which they were fighting.

☞ FOR THOSE WHO HAVE EVER COMPLAINED ABOUT A CONFUSING KNITTING PATTERN

A SOCK PATTERN, CIRCA 1800, WITH DIRECTIONS IN THEIR ENTIRETY:

For a child of ten cast on 72 stitches with Imperial knitting silk on three needles No. 16, and rib 1½ inch, 2 purl, 2 plain, then make 2 and knit 2 together for 1st row.

2nd row—Make 2, knit 1, letting the threads of the previous row drop, and always knitting the knitted stitch; care must be taken that each needle begins with the made stitch. Continue this until the stocking is the length required, then knit 6 rows plain into each stitch, and diminish for the toe; there will be 36 stitches every 9th stitch, 3 rows plain, then every 8th stitch, 2 rows plain, every 7th stitch, 1 row plain, then every row until only 12 stitches are left on the needles. Cast these off together leaving a rather square finish.

If a full sized stocking is required, 96 stitches must be cast on, or more if that is not large enough. The best guide for length is an old stocking that fits well.

● ● ● IF *LAMB FRIES* APPEARS ON THE MENU, be advised that the dish is made from a lamb's testicles that have usually been parboiled, cut, then seasoned.

∿ In Greek mythology, the hero Jason must find and retrieve a sheep's fleece made of gold in order to retake the throne from his uncle.

The Golden Fleece was kept in a land called Colchis, and was guarded by fire-breathing bulls and a dragon that never sleeps. Jason assembled a band of Greece's greatest heroes and sailed to Colchis on a boat called the *Argos*. Jason and his band of Argonauts undergo many trials and challenges as they endeavor to reclaim the fleece so that Jason can rightfully assume his throne.

Did you know that LEONARDO DA VINCI created a painting sometimes called *The Madonna of the Yarnwinder?*

• Also called *Madonna of the Spindles* (in Italian, *Madonna dei Fusi*), the oil painting was created in the early 16th century and features a seated Virgin Mary holding the Christ child. The Christ child is shown holding and gazing at a yarnwinder (nostepinne) or spindle. Many versions of the painting still exist, but the most famous are known as the *Buccleuch Madonna* (after its owner, the Scottish Duke of Buccleuch) and the *Lansdowne Madonna* (after its former owner, the Marquess of Lansdowne).

Scholars dispute whether and to what extent da Vinci actually had a hand in painting these two Madonnas, although the consensus is that one or both are at least partially from his hand, as opposed to being painted by his students. In 2003, The *Buccleuch Madonna* was the subject of a daring daytime robbery by thieves who brazenly carried the painting through a window of Scotland's Drumlanrig Castle in front of visiting tourists. However, the painting was recovered in 2007, and now hangs in the Scottish National Gallery.

{ THE CLEMSON COLLEGE SHEEP BARN
was built in the early 20th century and is listed in the National Register of Historic Places. It is the oldest surviving building relating to agriculture on the campus. }

⋙→ MATCH THE QUOTE

WITH THE KNITTING ICON WHO SAID IT.

KNITTING ICONS

A. Debbie Bliss
B. Alice Starmore
C. Elizabeth Zimmermann
D. Richard Rutt
E. Maggie Righetti
F. Barbara Walker
G. Kaffe Fassett
H. Mary Thomas
I. Montse Stanley
J. Priscilla Gibson-Roberts

● ● ●

1.

"In knitting there are ancient possibilities; the earth is enriched with the dust of the millions of knitters who have held wool and needles since the beginning of sheep."

2.

"There is something in every human soul which seeks to create a thing of beauty, given any sort of opportunity and materials to do so. . . . Knitting is very much a part of that age-old pursuit of the beautiful."

3.

"Knitting is best called a craft. It serves life and is relatively ephemeral. It gets worn and wears out (hence museum collections are sparse). It can be expensive, but is almost never precious. Its structure is more limiting than the structures of tapestry and embroidery. Therefore knitting is widely practiced by non-professionals and tends to be a people's craft."

4.

"The best periods of Knitting have always occurred when yarns have been scarce or expensive, as the desire for better knowledge of the work is stimulated in order that yarn need not be unduly wasted."

5.

"I hope you will experience, as I do, the deep pleasure of watching a colored pattern unfold as you knit from row to row. If it grabs you as it does me, you will discover that working one-color garments is quite monotonous by comparison."

6.

"Handknitting is a curiously cyclical activity. Periods in which it is fashionable to knit alternate with others in which the needles are left to grandmother."

7.

"I must have learned to knit when I was young but I have no childhood memories of a craft passed down by my mother—

rather of the royal-blue cardigan that she took out of the bag every autumn, knitted a few more rows of, then packed away in the spring. I had outgrown it long before it was completed!"

8.

"An egg can be served sunny-side up, over easy or scrambled, and it is still an egg. We all have our preferences about how eggs are served. . . . So it is with the construction of knitted items. We all have our favorite ways of making them: bottom up, top down, crosswise. Each way has its distinct advantages and serious drawbacks. Still they are hand-knits, just like eggs are eggs."

9.

"[I]t's amazing what you can do with a loop of yarn, if you take one loop, one idea, one technique at a time."

10.

"Someone without even a grain of mathematical ability can still possess a well-developed geometric sense, and can gain pleasure from a pattern, just as if it were a well-turned phrase in a novel or poem."

ANSWER KEY

6. I; 7. A; 8. E; 9. J; 10. B
1. C; 2. F; 3. D; 4. H; 5. G;

The term **SHEEPLE** refers to the tendency of human beings to follow the crowd without individual analysis, a combination of the words sheep and people.

A *spinster* is an unmarried woman, often considered past the typical age of marriage, and is a term to which many have a derogatory connotation today. Originally, it referred to a woman who spun thread or yarn, a common occupation for women in the middle ages, and was in use by the 14th century. Several hundred years later, the word had acquired a secondary meaning referring to an unmarried woman, perhaps because spinning was seen as the particular province of young, unmarried women living with their parents. Sometime after the beginning of the 18th century, the term acquired the "old maid" sense that it often connotes today. Note, however, that author Stephanie Coontz, in a study on marriage in society, suggests that spinster once had a proud and noble connotation, referring to women who earned their own living by spinning because they did not wish to marry.

The term *thrum* was originally a weaving term used to describe the short, loose ends of yarn that were left on the loom when a finished piece of weaving was cut away. *Thrumming* also refers to a method of using small tufts of yarn or roving by attaching them to knitting to create a dense and warm inner layer on mittens, hats, or even slippers and socks. The technique is sometimes called *tufting*, and it has been used for many years in Newfoundland and Labrador; folk mitten expert Marcia Lewandowski also identifies this technique as common in northern parts of Europe, such as Denmark. To add thrums to a piece of knitting, a knitter takes a precut length of yarn or roving and twists it, then knits the yarn or roving together with a stitch. Usually thrums are placed periodically throughout a knitted item; depending on gauge, a knitter may add tufts or thrums every 3 to 6 stitches on every 4th or 6th round. Thrums are sometimes knit so as to be invisible from the outside, and other times used to create patterns that show on the outside of the mitten or other item.

> IN ANCIENT ROME, woolen cloth was scoured or cleaned by submerging it in tubs of human urine. Slaves stood ankle-deep in the tubs and used their feet to stamp on the cloth.

Icelandic knitters are known for their lopapeysa (yoked sweaters), but a much older knitting tradition unique to Iceland is the knitted insole. Icelanders wore soft shoes made of skins, and they knitted beautiful insoles to add warmth to their shoes, which was necessary given the harsh climate. Although inserts were not visible when worn, they were made with great care, often using garter stitch, rose patterns, and as many as eight different colors within a single design. Icelandic knitters figured out how to knit insoles two or even four at a time in the round, finishing them with edging made of woven bands. While most inserts were made with straight edges, some were shaped to more closely fit the wearer's foot.

THE UNITED STATES POST OFFICE ISSUED A KNITTING-THEMED SET OF HOLIDAY STAMPS IN 2007. The set of four stamps featured winter images—a snowman, a reindeer, a snow-covered evergreen tree, and a teddy bear—created by machine knitter NANCY STAHL. Stahl originally designed the images using computer software, then she transferred the designs to an electronic knitting machine. The first set of knitted images didn't look right, so Stahl concluded the gauge was too tight. She converted the designs for use on a different knitting machine and was pleased with the images once the stitches were larger. She then scanned the images and did some retouching before they were finished. The face value of the stamps was 41 cents. Savvy stitchers may also recall a needlepoint stamp, issued in 1973, featuring a Christmas tree designed by needlepoint artist Dolli Tingle, the first of several needlepoint-themed stamps issued by the US Post Office.

In spring 2014, athletic shoe company Adidas premiered the world's first knit sneaker. Called *Primeknit*, the limited-edition shoe was the first to have an upper that was completely knit from heel to toe. Adidas described the knit shoe as "providing a bespoke second-skin fit that retains the strength of a conventional boot." The Primeknit was made without any textile waste and featured "zones" that were knit at different gauges and with different stitches to cater to the needs of the athlete. Yarn used to create the Primeknit received a special water-resistant coating. Retail price at the time of launch: around $350.

THE BRITISH WOOL MARKETING BOARD, begun in 1950 to promote the best possible return for producers of wool, is the only remaining agricultural commodity board in the UK.

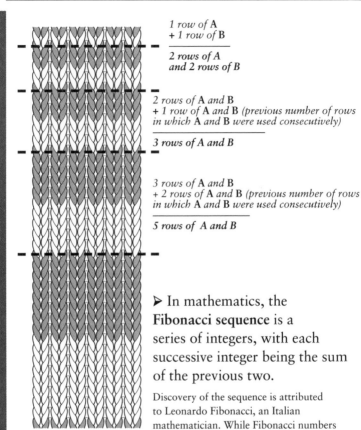

1 row of **A**
+ 1 row of **B**

2 rows of A
and 2 rows of B

2 rows of A and B
+ 1 row of **A** *and* **B** *(previous number of rows*
in which **A** *and* **B** *were used consecutively)*

3 rows of A and B

3 rows of **A** *and* **B**
+ 2 rows of **A** *and* **B** *(previous number of rows*
in which **A** *and* **B** *were used consecutively)*

5 rows of A and B

➤ In mathematics, the **Fibonacci sequence** is a series of integers, with each successive integer being the sum of the previous two.

Discovery of the sequence is attributed to Leonardo Fibonacci, an Italian mathematician. While Fibonacci numbers are important in a variety of mathematical and scientific contexts, it's also believed that they can be applied to the visual arts to create patterns that are aesthetically appealing. One of the most common applications is to create stripes in a Fibonacci-derived sequence, knitting first 1 row of color A, then 2 rows of color B, then 3 rows of color A, then 5 rows of color B, and so on; or by repeating the sequence in each color (1 row of A, 1 row of B; 2 rows of A, 2 rows of B; 3 rows of A, 3 rows of B; and so on). Using a predetermined pattern like the Fibonacci sequence is an easy alternative to knitting equal-sized stripes or random stripes (which are hard to truly randomize given the brain's tendency to create regular patterns).

In Greek mythology, a *chimera* was a monster that was part lion, part snake, and part goat. Today, geneticists are creating something similar by taking genetic material from an orb-weaver spider and combining it with the DNA of a goat's udder. The combined material is then added to the cells of a goat embryo, which in turn, is implanted into a female goat. The resulting offspring produces spider silk protein in her milk—spider silk that can be extracted and used to spin fiber that has many of the same properties as spider's silk created by spiders. It's stronger than a steel wire of the same circumference and can be stretched without losing its strength. Researchers hope that spider silk fibers can be produced and harvested for such varied uses as medical sutures, bulletproof vests, biodegradable fishing line, and super-strong parachutes. If scientists figure out a way to produce spider silk in greater quantity, who knows—some day spider-silk yarn may be available in yarn stores around the world.

●●●

WHO WAS
SUSAN BATES,
AND DID SHE REALLY MAKE KNITTING NEEDLES?

Actually, there was no real Susan Bates. The original name of the Susan Bates company was C.J. BATES & SON. When the company needed a name for its line of needlework implements, "Susan Bates" was chosen with the hope of creating an iconic brand name like Betty Crocker.

THE FIRST RECORDED SHEEPDOG TRIALS IN THE UNITED STATES WERE HELD IN PHILADELPHIA IN 1880 as part of the International Exhibition of Sheep, Wool and Wool Products. Four dogs competed. The test, according to the *Philadelphia Inquirer*, "was the driving of five sheep from a pen in the northwestern corner of the yard around the track and penning them in another enclosure." First prize was awarded to a dog named Tom, owned by a Charles Pugh.

SOCK KNITTERS USUALLY FINISH THE TOE
OF A HAND-KNITTED SOCK USING A GRAFTING
TECHNIQUE CALLED *KITCHENER STITCH.*
The technique is named after Lord Horatio Herbert Kitchener, born in
1850 in Ireland, who became a military strategist and served in various
capacities in Khartoum, Sudan, Egypt, India, and South Africa. In
1914, Kitchener was named Secretary of State for War. Unlike many
strategists and politicians of his time, Kitchener was convinced World War I would last for a long time, and he made preparations accordingly. His likeness was featured on one of the most famous recruitment posters of all time, originally published on the cover of *London Opinion* magazine.

• • • • • • •

Kitchener is also reportedly the inventor of the grafting technique that still bears his name; knitting lore says that he created a new way to fasten the toes of socks so as not to create a thick seam that could irritate the toes of soldiers.

∿TYPES OF SPINDLES

From a structural standpoint, there are three types of spindles
distinguished by the placement of the whorl, the round disc that is
used to weight the spindle and keep it spinning.

■ TOP (OR HIGH) WHORL
SPINDLES have a whorl
that is near the top of the shaft.

■ BOTTOM (OR LOW)
WHORL SPINDLES
have a whorl near the bottom
of the shaft.

■ SUPPORTED SPINDLES
have the whorl in the middle
of the shaft.

Both top and bottom whorl spindles
are commonly called drop spindles
since they are suspended when
used—the spindle spins in the air
and is "dropped" or hung from
the newly twisted yarn. Supported
spindles must be placed against
an object when spinning with them
because the weight of the spindle
is too great to suspend it in the air
while in use.

THE KNITTING NANCY
HAS MANY ALIASES:
knitting dolly, knitting
mushroom, **Bizzy Lizzie**,
peg knitter, knitting spool,
knitting noddy, **knitting tower**,
French knitter
(or French knitting machine),
knitting knob, corker,
tricotin (France),
strickliesel (Germany),
dolly bobbin.

THE GODDESS
OF YARN

In Latvian mythology,
Dziparu-māte
(sometimes known as Dzparina
Mamulina) was a type of
mother-goddess of yarn.
Latvian mythology recognized
Dieves as the male god,
while Māte was his female
counterpart; other Latvian
goddesses were considered
assistants or alternative faces of
Māte. Dziparu-māte (translated
variously as "yarn mother"
or "mother of colored wool")
was called upon by knitters to
watch over their yarn and make
sure it didn't tangle.

☞ Based on a 2013 trade industry survey,
the average knitter spent $801 in the past 12 months
on fiber arts supplies, with a median of $500.
Two percent of respondents reported spending more than $4000
on supplies for the past year. Now that's a stash!

THREE BAGS FULL,
by Leonie Swann,
is a **mystery novel** that
is told entirely from the
perspective of a
flock of sheep that
investigates when their
shepherd is found dead,
stabbed by a shovel.

⇛➜ During World War I,
a British company
marketed a canvas sock
measurer called the
"Man in Khaki
Sock-Knitter's Help."
It was designed to make
measuring various segments
of a sock easier, with knitting
for the troops in mind.

In 19th-century France, a man named Sylvain Dornon walked from Paris to Moscow in 58 days. Although the time frame is in and of itself impressive, it's especially amazing when you consider that Dornon walked on stilts the entire way.

Dornon was from the Gascony region of France, where the ground frequently became marshy and nearly impassable by foot after rains. The inhabitants of this area began using stilts to move around—in particular shepherds tending flocks that were spread out over a large area. The stilts were about five feet tall and called tchangues, or "big legs." A shepherd could become so skilled at walking on stilts that he could knit, spin, or even pick something up from the ground without getting off them.

A S OF MID-2014, Technorati, a now defunct website dedicated to searching and indexing blogs, pulled up nearly **3,000 blogs** identified as relating to knitting (2,990, to be precise). That's more knitting-related blogs than those relating to golf (2,944), beer (2,763), comic books (1,060), oil painting (659), crochet (1,362), hand spinning (a mere 20!), and, curiously, yarn (932). ■ ■ ■ ■

At the 1893 World's Fair in Chicago, the New South

Wales portion of Australia's exhibit featured pyramidal displays made of bales of wool, a wall of wool, and large signage prominently displaying statistics about Australia's wool industry. One viewer stated,

> *"No other country had such a display, and it was universally acknowledged to be the finest and best arranged in the Agricultural Building."*

☛ TRADE CARDS WERE A FORM OF PRINTED ADVERTISING POPULAR IN VICTORIAN TIMES.

THE FIRST TRADE CARDS were created by businesses in 18th century England to advertise their wares, and they included maps to direct customers to their shops since there was no formal street numbering system in use at the time. With the rise of lithography in the 1870s, trade cards could be mass-produced and became wildly popular. Usually a trade card featured an image of some kind on one side, with an advertisement or other information about a merchant or business on the other. In the early 20th century, trade cards became more expensive than advertising in magazines and newspapers, and they fell out of use. Today, collectors seek out these small printed cards,

with some rare cards sold at auction for hundreds or even thousands of dollars. Of course, yarn and thread manufacturers were among the companies who used trade cards. One trade card published by the Eureka Silk Manufacturing Company was titled "To Our Lady Customers" and observed, *"The Art of Knitting is now considered a desirable accomplishment by every lady in the land."* Women knitting, particularly in rocking chairs by the fire, were a popular motif, as were cats playing with balls of yarn. ∾

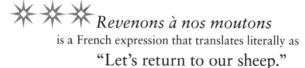

✳ ✳ ✳ *Revenons à nos moutons*
is a French expression that translates literally as
"Let's return to our sheep."

The expression is used when a speaker digresses from the topic at hand, to mean "let's return to the original subject." It was first used in a medieval play called *La Farce de Maître Pierre Pathelin*, in which the dishonest title character tries to confuse a judge by bringing two lawsuits: one concerning sheep, and one concerning sheets or cloth.

The wily advocate brings up the latter in order to distract the judge, causing the judge to repeatedly say, "Revenons à nos moutons."

⟫⟫→TIMELINE OF SWEATER FASHION

A warm winter knit will always be in style, as evidenced by the plethora of popular sweaters throughout the last century.

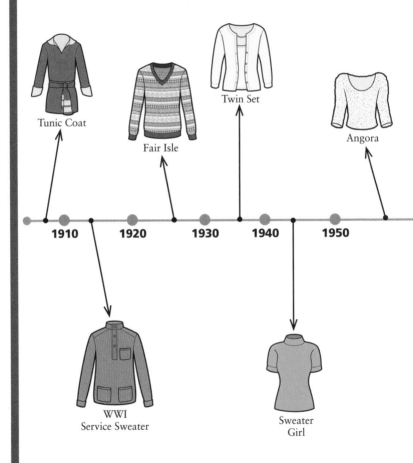

Tunic Coat

Fair Isle

Twin Set

Angora

1910   **1920**   **1930**   **1940**   **1950**

WWI
Service Sweater

Sweater
Girl

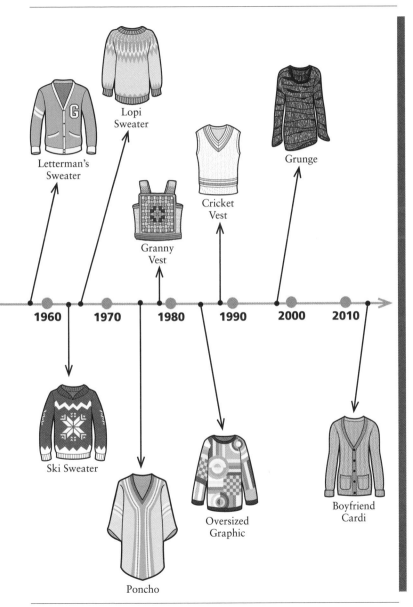

Letterman's Sweater

Lopi Sweater

Granny Vest

Cricket Vest

Grunge

1960   1970   1980   1990   2000   2010

Ski Sweater

Poncho

Oversized Graphic

Boyfriend Cardi

ACKNOWLEDGEMENTS

>>>→ FIRST AND MOST IMPORTANT: thanks to Trisha Malcolm, friend, partner-in-crime, and mentor. We cooked up the idea for this book at lunch one day, proving that only good things come when friends get together. Thank you for seeing the potential in the concept and helping turn it into a project of which I am very proud.

Thanks to Linda Roghaar, my trusty agent, and my friends at Lark Crafts/Sterling Publishing, for helping work out the contractual details that allowed me to work with Sixth&Spring on this project. ■ ■ ■ ■

Although I worked with several different editors at various points (including Joy Aquilino and Kristina McGowan), Laura Cooke deserves great thanks for stepping in mid-river and helming this ship to the other side. Diane Lamphron was a wonder, creating a lovely design that perfectly captures the spirit of the book. Deepest appreciation to fact checker Betty Christiansen, who helped keep me honest, and everyone else at Sixth&Spring who helped make the book happen, in particular, Art Joinnides for greenlighting this untraditional knitting book.

Thanks to all of the knitters and industry insiders who suggested factoids and tidbits for me to explore. Thanks to Cotton Incorporated and The Woolmark Company for granting permission to reproduce their wonderful logos.

➤ I simply would not have survived the past year without my dear friends. *Brooke, Elizabeth, Kathy, Laura G., Laura M., Pat, Patty, Trisha, Véronik,* and my longest and best friend, *my mom.* Thank you for always being ready to take a tearful call or laugh at a silly anecdote. I would not be here were it not for your support.

> And of course, thanks to
> *my dear family* for putting up with my
> endless tendency to prattle on about yarn
> and sheep and metric tons of fiber.

BIBLIOGRAPHY

A book of this scope necessarily has drawn from many sources, but if you're interested in learning more about some of the topics I've touched on, allow me to recommend the following:

Bush, Nancy.
Folk Socks.
Loveland, CO: Interweave 2012.

Falick, Melanie.
Knitting In America.
New York:
Artisan 1996.

Fournier, Elizabeth and Nola Fournier. *In Sheep's Clothing.*
Loveland, CO: (Interweave 2013.

Hiatt, June Hemmons.
The Principles of Knitting.
New York: Touchstone 2012.

Lewandoski, Marcia.
Folk Mittens.
Loveland, CO: Interweave 2013.

MacDonald, Anne.
No Idle Hands: The Social History of American Knitting.
New York: Ballantine 1990.

Oberle, Cheryl.
Folk Shawls.
Loveland, CO: Interweave 2000.

Parkes, Clara.
The Knitter's Book of Wool.
New York: Potter Craft 2007.

Parkes, Clara.
The Knitter's Book of Yarn . New York: Potter Craft 2009

Perry, Barbara.
Adventures in Yarn Farming.
Boston: Roost, 2013.

Righetti, Maggie.
Knitting In Plain English.
New York: St. Martin's 2007.

Rutt, Richard.
A History of Handknitting.
Loveland, CO: Interweave 1989.

Smith, Beth Shearer.
The Spinner's Book of Fleece.
Boston: Roost 2013.

Thomas, Mary.
Mary Thomas's Knitting Book .
Mineola, NY: Dover 1972.

Vogue Knitting Magazine, Ed.
The Best of Vogue Knitting Magazine.
New York: Sixth & Spring 2007).

Vogue Knitting Magazine, Ed.
Vogue Knitting Knitopedia.
New York: Sixth & Spring 2011.

Walker, Barbara.
Knitting From the Top. Pittsville, WI: Schoolhouse Press 1996.

Zimmermann, Elizabeth.
Knitting Without Tears.
New York: Fireside Books 1973
[Don't stop there; read everything she ever wrote.—CK]

INDEX

A

acronyms 44
Adidas Primeknit 121
afghans 18
airplanes, knitting needles on 70
Alcatraz 33
alpacas 14, 56
angora 28
arborglyphs 65
argyle 87
Arkwright, Richard 33
artwork 46, 117
Australia 85, 126

B

balaclavas 10, 99
bellwethers 104
black sheep 54, 103
Black Sheep Squadron 69
Black Sheep sweaters 54
Blake, William 110
blogs 126
Bohus knitting 110
books 16, 81, 84, 101, 125
Boye, James H. 47
Boyington, Gregory "Pappy" 69
Brooks Brothers 11
broomstick lace 98
Buchanan, James 31
buffaloes 56
bumper stickers 64, 83

C

Cabbage Patch Kids 85
camels 56, 104
Catherine the Great 7
celebrity knitters 52, 54, 95
center-pull balls 54
charts, knitting 86
China 91, 92
chullos 61
Clemson College Sheep
  Barn 117
clocks 26, 58
college courses 73
color cards 15
colors 14, 19, 60, 65, 78–79, 83

Columbia University 30
competitions 11, 97
Coolidge, Grace 77
cotton 68, 91, 109
crafting get-togethers 49
crochet 14, 39, 59, 98–99
crochet hooks 7, 19, 33, 111
crochet knitting machines 45
crochet needles 19
cross-breeds 91

D

The Dark Knight Rises 94
"The Darning Needle"
  (Andersen) 54
da Vinci, Leonardo 117
days, yarn-related 40
Diana, Princess 54
Dickens, Charles 38, 94
diseases of fiber producers 92
DK-weight yarn 114
Dolly (sheep) 76
"Duffy and the Devil" 35
dyestuffs, unusual 18

E

Ennis, Grace 55
Eucalan 95

F

Fassett, Kaffe 72, 105, 112
Feather & Fan 108–109
feet, largest 17
felting 36
Fibonacci sequence 122
filet crochet 99
fleece-to-garment competition 97
folklore 14, 35, 53, 54,
  116, 125
Ford, Gerald R. 69
French Revolution 38
fulling 36

G

Gandhi, Mahatma 87
garters, knitted 60
Gauguin, Jane 57

goats 56, 86
goddess of yarn 125
Godey's Lady's Book 107
Golden Fleece 116
Golden Fleece logo 11
Golden Shears competition 11
Great Britain 93, 102, 106, 121
Guernsey sweaters 104
guilds 102
Gunnister Man 103

H
hairpin lace/crochet 99
hats, whimsical 72
heathered yarns 78
Heindselman's 51
hemp 49
Henry IV (king of France) 67
Her Excellency's Knitting Book
(Liverpool) 81
Herzog, Amy 112
holiday sweaters, tacky 74
home knitting ban 83

I
Iceland 71, 120
indigo 73
insoles, knitted 120
Irish crochet/lace 99

J
jokes 20
jumpers 76

K
King Charles Brocade 39
King Philip's War 90
Kitchener stitch 124
knickerbockers 82
KnitList 44
knitted lace 39
knitter in residence 26
knitting. *see also specific topics*
  accessories/tools 24–25
  calories burned by 48
  charts 86
  invention of 21
  items, unusual 36
  mystery novels 16

projects, top 63
supply purchases 125
terms 32, 59, 106
knitting cups 34
knitting machines 45, 66–67, 85
Knitting Nancy 125
knitting needles
  on airplanes 70
  circular, interchangeable 52
  conversion chart 84
  folklore 14
  largest 7
  light-up 13
  materials in 63
  U.S. manufacturer, first 33
knitting shops 113
Kraemer Yarns 107
Kubrick, Stanley 75

L
lace knitting 39, 77
Lambert, Frances 57
lamb fries 116
lanolin 111
Lee, William 66–67
license plates 105
Lincoln, Abraham 42
llamas 14, 56, 71
logos 11, 31, 109
lopapeysa 71
Luddite riots 85

M
Macdonald, Hugh 106
The Madonna of the Yarnwinder
(da Vinci) 117
magazines 19, 101, 112. see also
  Vogue Knitting
marathon/knitting record 28
marled yarn 78
Mary, Queen 106
Mary Maxim company 9
Mary Rose (ship) 53
measurements, common 34
Mee, Cornelia 57
Merino sheep 99
Midnight Cowboy 72
miners 17
mistakes 45, 81

mittens 43, 53
Möbius strips 104
mohair 40, 73
monks 30, 68
movies 74, 75, 94, 109, 113
mule-spun yarn 97
musk oxen 8, 11, 56
mutton busting 39
mystery novels 16, 125

N
Naked Sheep Wines 114
namesakes 93
Navajo-Churro sheep 83
needle gauges 37
nepps 111
New Zealand 81, 85, 97, 114
Nicnevin 53
Noro, Eisaku 81
Norwegian knitting 41
nupps 111
nylon 9

O
Old English Sheepdog 75
Old Shale 108–109
ombré yarns 79
Order of the Golden Fleece 48
Orenburg shawls 7

P
patron saint 6–7
patterns 57, 81, 116
penguin sweaters 74–75
Pennsylvania 69
Philip the Good 48
Pinckney, Eliza Lucas 73
pita lace 63
Pleasant Valley War 17
pompoms 28
possum, brushtail 18
proverbs 12
purl stitch 105
purses, relic 42

Q
qiviut 8
quotes 23, 100–101, 118–119

R
rabbits 56
ragg yarns 78
raglan sleeves 15
Ravelry 14, 68, 72
rayon 47
"Revenons à nos moutons" 127
rhymes 96
Richard the Lionheart 68
Riego de la Branchardière,
Eléonore 57
Rinker, Molly "Mom" 50
Rome, ancient 120
ROWAN magazine 19, 112
Rowlandson, Mary 90

S
sailors 25
Schlesinger, John 72
Seal of Cotton logo 109
Selbu knitting 41, 53
self-patterning yarns 78
self-striping yarns 79
shawls 7, 21
sheep. see also wool;
    specific types
  anatomy 27, 90
  breeds 92, 115
  cloned 76
  consumption of 85
  counting 31, 65
  dyed 111
  expensive 35
  eyeball as hangover cure 53
  facts 10
  family feud over 17
  Great Britain 102
  as mascots 90
  mating 86
  nomenclature 56
  North America 32
  as oracle 105
  poem 110
  population 48
  proverbs 12
  soccer match 44
  teeth compared to 97
  wool 39, 51, 68
  words from behavior of 106